YOUR BRAIN'S NOT BROKEN

FOR TEENS AND YOUNG ADULTS

Books by Tamara Rosier

Your Brain's Not Broken

Your Brain's Not Broken Workbook

You, Me, and Our ADHD Family

YOUR BRAIN'S NOT BROKEN

FOR TEENS AND YOUNG ADULTS

Strategies for your Life with ADHD

TAMARA ROSIER, PHD

Revell
a division of Baker Publishing Group
Grand Rapids, Michigan

Published by Revell
a division of Baker Publishing Group
Grand Rapids, Michigan
RevellBooks.com

Printed in the United States of America

Library of Congress Cataloging-in-Publication Data

Names: Rosier, Tamara, 1968– author

Title: Your brain's not broken for teens and young adults : strategies for your life with adhd / Tamara Rosier.

Description: Grand Rapids, Michigan : Revell, a division of Baker Publishing Group, 2026. | Includes bibliographical references. | Audience: Ages 12–20

Identifiers: LCCN 2025048652 | ISBN 9780800747565 paperback | ISBN 9781493455621 ebook

Subjects: LCSH: Attention-deficit hyperactivity disorder in adolescence | Attention-deficit hyperactivity disorder in adolescence—Treatment | Anxiety in adolescence | JUVENILE FICTION / General Classification: LCC RJ506.H9 .R6665 2026 | DDC 618.92/8589—dc23/eng/20260505

LC record available at https://lccn.loc.gov/2025048652

The names and details of the people and situations described in this book have been changed or presented in composite form in order to ensure the privacy of those with whom the author has worked.

Baker Publishing Group publications use paper produced from sustainable forestry practices and postconsumer waste whenever possible.

26 27 28 29 30 31 32 7 6 5 4 3 2 1

To my teen and young adult clients.
You've taught me so much.
I hope I represented your stories well.

Dear Parent,

One December evening, my daughter turned to me during *Rudolph the Red-Nosed Reindeer* and said, "I feel like I'm on the Island of Misfit Toys." On the screen, a menagerie of darling but slightly different toys danced around: a spotted elephant, a train with square wheels, and a bird that swam instead of flew.

My daughter was in second grade, and it was becoming apparent that school would be difficult for her. She wasn't disrespectful or unruly. Instead, she was a lot like the water pistol that squirted jelly in the movie. She was a *misfit* toy who did not seem to fit others' expectations. She consistently missed her teacher's cues and paid for it with verbal scolding and points taken away. Instead of loving recess like other children, she hated it. She felt completely overwhelmed in the hallway, watching her friends scurry to put on their snow pants and winter gear before racing outside for play. She forgot and lost oh so many things at school and at home. Her observation about being on the Island of Misfit Toys confirmed to me that all the negative attention was beginning to take a toll on her.

Children with ADHD know they are different, and this is rarely experienced as a good thing. They often develop low self-esteem because they realize they make mistakes, like not finishing what they start, misunderstanding directions, or losing their mittens for the fifth time that winter. And because children make no distinction between what they do and who they are, they often feel less capable than their peers. Like the toy bird that swam instead of flew, they can feel as though they don't belong—out of place in a world that seems built for a different kind of wiring, quietly wondering why something that looks so easy for everyone else feels so hard for them.

And then they grow into teens and young adults. The playground missteps turn into missed deadlines. The misplaced mittens become misplaced assignments, lost jobs, or forgotten responsibilities. The scolding shifts from teachers to bosses or friends. That same sense of being a "misfit toy" can follow them into bigger, harder spaces where the cost feels even higher.

What your child needs most is not for you to "fix the toy" but for you to be with them on the island. To sit next to them, see their world through their eyes, and remind them they are lovable, capable, and not alone.

This book is written for teens and young adults first. The tone, examples, and strategies are designed to speak directly to them in their own world. It's not meant to be read *to* them or used *against* them. It's meant to be their companion—a book they can read on their own, underline, argue with, or return to when life feels overwhelming.

Your role is to support their journey. If they share something from the book, listen with curiosity. If they don't, respect that privacy. Trust that even when they roll their eyes, they're noticing more than you think.

From years of working with families, I've learned that children with ADHD who thrive aren't the ones raised in homes with perfectly color-coded chore charts, polished executive function hacks, or the cleanest rooms. They are the ones whose parents build a strong, safe relationship that helps their child grow resilience and self-efficacy.

The most significant thing you can do for your child is to create a durable, healthy relationship with them. Four characteristics create that relationship:

- *Endless empathy:* seeing your child's feelings as real, even when they come out big and messy.
- *Trusting respect:* treating your child with dignity and modeling the same behavior you want from them.
- *Stubborn love:* showing a love that does not waver, even when their behavior is not what you want.
- *Gentle honesty:* offering feedback at the right time, in a way that builds trust instead of tearing it down.

If you hold on to these qualities, you give your child something no strategy or system can replace: the confidence that they are deeply loved, worthy of respect, and capable of writing their own story.

This book is their tool. You are their safe place. Together, those two things can change how they see themselves and how they step into the world.

Contents

Preface

Dear Brilliant, Distracted, Determined Human,

Your brain's not broken. But I know it can feel that way sometimes. ADHD has a way of making even simple things–turning in an assignment, answering a text, starting a project–feel like forty-seven tabs open in your brain at once. You want to do better, but starting can feel impossible.

Maybe you've already tried strategies that didn't stick. Each time they fell apart, it felt like proof you'd never figure things out. If that sounds familiar, you're not alone.

If you've ever wondered whether a book like this could actually help, here's why it might be worth your time:

- Move past being told to "just focus" or "try harder" when you're already doing your best.
- Get tools that work *with* your brain, not against it.
- Understand why procrastination, forgetting, and overwhelm keep showing up–and what to do about them.
- Turn your creativity, humor, and big ideas into real strengths.
- Figure out who you are and what really matters to you.

This book is meant to walk with you through this process. You can move through it in your own way–skip around, mark it up, question it, or come back later. What matters is that it belongs to you.

And while ADHD is part of your story, it isn't the whole story. You get to decide what comes next.

I'm glad you're here.

Tamara

1

"Why Can't I Just . . . ?"

"I don't know what's wrong with me," she said.

A college freshman, Abbi sat across from me—bright, thoughtful, exhausted. Her knees were tucked on the chair, her sleeve twisting through her fingers, as if she needed something solid to hold.

"I missed my nine a.m. again. I set my alarm, I swear. Last night I planned to finish my reading, write a few paragraphs, text my roommate about dinner. Instead, I reorganized my Google Drive for two hours, panicked, and froze."

Abbi shook her head and talked even faster. "I get good grades. But I never sleep. I miss deadlines even when I care. I forget my charger, my keys, my lunch—everything." She paused and then added, "But sometimes I remember too much. I replay that awkward thing I said to a guy I'm talking to. Oh, and I still haven't answered a bunch of DMs. At this point it feels awkward to even text back—it's been so long."

Abbi looked up for a second, testing the air between us: *Are you going to tell me the same thing everyone else does?* She didn't have to say it out loud. She was waiting for me to tell her to try harder. Instead, she said preemptively, "I try. I try so hard. But my brain just doesn't do what I need it to do."

She wasn't making excuses. She was trying to decode a brain that kept short-circuiting in a world built for smooth performance. From the outside, she looked fine. Maybe even impressive. But on the inside, her brain felt chaotic.

"I feel like I'm failing at stuff that shouldn't be hard. Like everyone else got a 'how to human' handbook and I missed it," she added.

"That makes sense," I told her. "You're working hard. But your brain works differently. And nobody sees that part. They see the late paper, the unanswered texts, the emotional moments that get misread as drama."

She nodded. "Like I'm out of sync with everyone."

ADHD can feel like that. And it's draining.

Abbi's effort was real. Her energy, her planning, her trying—it was all real. But when the outcome didn't match the effort, she filled in the blank with a story that blamed herself. And that's when the shame-filled questions started creeping in: *Why can't I just do life better? Or stop this thing? Or keep it together like everyone else seems to?*

When your brain doesn't understand *why* something is difficult, it tends to make up a story—and that story usually points the finger at you. ADHD brains are wired differently. Without the right support, that wiring can turn everyday challenges into shame spirals. The issue isn't who you are; it's how your brain handles three things: motivation, feedback, and emotions. And once you understand that, you can actually work with it.

Maybe Abbi's story feels familiar. Maybe it doesn't. ADHD doesn't come with one look or one story.

ADHD can feel like forty-seven tabs open—every one autoplaying. Or it's like walking through mud: You know the steps, but your feet won't move. Sometimes it's both at once: racing and stopping, wired and tired.

When you know the common patterns of ADHD, it's easier to make sense of your own experiences. Instead of thinking, *What's wrong with me?*, you can start to see, *Oh, that's part of how ADHD works.* Let's look at a few of the most common ADHD patterns. These don't cover everything, but they'll give you a picture of how ADHD can show up in daily life.

Trouble with Focus (But Not the Way People Think)

People often think ADHD means you can't pay attention. That's not quite right. ADHD is really about *attention regulation*—your brain doesn't always lock onto what's important. Instead, it reacts to whatever's interesting, emotional, urgent, or distracting in the moment.

Jayden, a high school junior, put it this way: "I had a plan. A real one. Finish bio reading, outline my essay, and email my teacher before dinner. I had a quiet room, white noise, snacks, and the document open. Then I checked a text. And that led to a meme. Then I jumped into a rabbit hole about whether sharks sleep." By the time he remembered an email from another teacher, it was almost midnight and nothing on his list was done. He panicked and ended up watching a video about making steel.

Jayden wasn't being irresponsible. He knew what to do. ADHD researcher Russell Barkley explains that ADHD is a performance disorder, not a knowledge disorder.* Doing

* Russell Barkley, "ADHD as a Disorder of Performance, Not Knowledge," posted August 8, 2023, by Russell Barkley, YouTube, 16 min., 40 sec., https://www.youtube.com/watch?v=58gU8tsxkkl.

Quick Definitions

Task initiation: getting yourself to start something even when you don't feel like it.

Self-regulation: steering your thoughts, feelings, and actions so you can finish what you start

something *on time*, *on purpose*—especially when it's boring or emotionally loaded—is the hard part.

To others, it can look like Jayden wasn't trying. Other people might say:

- "You need to focus."
- "You're smart—you could do this if you really cared."
- "You're careless."

Jayden wasn't choosing to drift. His attention was chasing stimulation, like a radio scanning through every channel at once. When everything feels equally important—a paper, an email, a meme, and whether sharks sleep—his focus bounces instead of sticking to what matters most.

For a lot of people with ADHD, the problem isn't effort. It's that starting feels impossible—and once you finally get going, your brain might swing the other way and refuse to let go.

Hyperfocus (Or, Why You Can Spend Six Hours on *Minecraft* but Can't Seem to Start Your Essay)

One confusing part of ADHD is that sometimes you focus so hard that hours disappear. Tasha, a high school senior, sat down to sketch before reviewing her history flash cards.

"I opened my sketchbook," she said, "and then the rest of the world disappeared. I didn't eat dinner. I didn't even get up to use the bathroom. When my sister walked in, she asked if I was okay because I hadn't spoken in hours. I was totally into my drawing."

That's hyperfocus–your mind locks onto something and refuses to let go. Time? Gone. Hunger? Paused. From the outside, it can look obsessive or avoidant. Your brain just hit a dopamine jackpot, dropping you into a focus trance.

With ADHD, the question isn't whether you can focus; it's what captures your attention and whether you can shift it on purpose. You can't always choose when hyperfocus shows up, but you can choose what to do when you realize that it has happened.

ADHD isn't only about locking in too hard. Sometimes it's the opposite–you can't sit still, even when your brain is out of gas. That's restlessness.

Restlessness (Or, When Your Body Has the Zoomies but Your Brain Is Out of Gas)

Restlessness doesn't always look like bouncing off the walls. It can be a knee jitter under the table, sleeves getting tugged, or scroll-refresh-scroll. It can be pacing at midnight or color-coding notes instead of studying them. Sometimes it's invisible: a pressure under your skin like tiny electric currents, even when you're still.

Leo, a college sophomore, said, "Even when I'm exhausted, my brain's like, 'What's next? What are we forgetting?' I'll stand up, sit down, walk around, and open the fridge five times. Half the time I don't notice until someone points it out."

Restlessness is what happens when the body stays in motion long after the brain is tired. Other people might see it and say:

- "You're so fidgety."
- "You need to learn to relax."
- "Why are you always moving?"

What they may not understand is that movement can be a response to internal overload—your body's way of restoring balance when everything inside feels like too much.

Sometimes the energy spills outward as movement. Other times it stays inside—a swarm of thoughts and sounds fighting for first place. And when everything is yelling for attention at the same time, people mistake that for not paying attention.

Distractibility (Or, When a Sound or a Sudden Thought Can Hijack Your Mind)

People assume distractibility means that you can't pay attention. Instead, it's like your brain tries to pay attention to *everything*—all at once. The conversation next to you, the fly in the window, the buzzing lights, the tag in your shirt, that one cringy thing you said in sixth grade—it all comes crashing into your head at once.

Cameron, a high school sophomore, told me about his English class. "I liked the book! But then my brain jumped to how the teacher's shoes squeaked, which reminded me of gym class, which reminded me of dodgeball in seventh grade, which reminded me of that meme with the flying shoe. And suddenly we were on the next chapter."

Distractibility also comes from *inside*: thoughts stealing the mic. Luna, one of my middle school clients, practices catching herself and says, "Oh wait, my brain forgot to listen.

Can you say that last part again?" She laughed when she told me this and added, "My mom doesn't love that. But at least I noticed!"

Other people might see you getting distracted and say:

- "You never listen."
- "Stop daydreaming and pay attention."

They don't see how much energy it takes to stay present when your mind keeps changing the subject.

And a distracted brain doesn't always pause before it reacts. One second you're thinking it, the next second it's already out of your mouth or in a text you wish you hadn't sent. That's impulsivity.

Impulsivity (Or, Oops, I Said It Before I Thought It)

Eli, a high school sophomore, sighed. "My friend was joking–normal stuff–and I made a comment that sounded . . . mean. I wasn't mad. It just came out. Now it's weird between us."

Impulsivity can be blurting the answer, spending your whole paycheck on an Amazon order, sending a text the second you think of it, or saying yes before you've decided.

With ADHD, the way you're wired leans toward action first, reflection later. That pause-before-you-leap moment can be super short–or missing entirely. Sometimes you don't even realize what happened until afterward, when you're figuring out how to clean up the mess.

Other people might see impulsivity and say:

- "You're so rude."
- "You're so immature."
- "Get a filter."

Your brain's action system moves faster than the filter system. And impulsivity doesn't only affect your actions or attention. With ADHD, emotions can move just as quickly, showing up before there's time to pause or think.

Emotional Intensity (Or, When You Feel Everything All at Once)

ADHD doesn't only shape attention; it shapes emotion–how fast feelings arrive, how strong they hit, and how long they hang around.

Sasha sat across from me, eyes red. During a group project, a classmate had rolled her eyes and muttered something. Sasha wasn't even sure the actions were meant for her, yet they landed as if they were. Heat rushed to her face; her stomach dropped; her hands shook. Minutes later she was crying in the bathroom, overwhelmed and humiliated. "I know I shouldn't care this much," she whispered. "It wasn't even a big deal. But I felt it . . . all at once."

From the outside, people may say:

- "You're overreacting."
- "Calm down."
- "It's not that deep."

Your emotions aren't wrong. They're real and powerful. We'll unpack the mechanics–why reactions can jump from 0 to 10 and how to steady them–in chapter 3. For now, know this: Intensity is part of the system, and you can learn to steer it.

Looking at Your Own Patterns

Hyperfocus, restlessness, distractibility, impulsivity, and emotional intensity may look different on the outside, but they all trace back to the same source: a brain that processes life at full volume. When your brain runs that loud, even small things can feel huge—exciting, frustrating, or both at once.

It's one thing to read about ADHD traits; it's another to recognize them in yourself. The quiz on the following pages helps you do that. It's not for diagnosing ADHD; it's just a mirror to help you see patterns in your own life.

For each statement, choose the option that fits you best: *very often*, *sometimes*, or *hardly ever*. Go with what feels most true in your day-to-day life, not just how you feel on a good day or a bad one. Don't overthink it—trust your first reaction and keep moving.

- Start by looking at the boxes you checked.
- Do certain areas cluster together—like focus and memory, or emotions and sensitivity?
- Which ones seem to trip you up the most right now?
- Are there any that surprised you?

Now try getting another perspective. Ask a parent, sibling, or close friend to glance at the list and share what they notice. Sometimes the people around us can point out patterns we miss. Be clear that you're not asking for criticism; you're asking for insight. You could say something like:

- "These are things I'm trying to notice in myself. Which ones sound most like me to you?"
- "Do you see times when these traits help me, or when they make things harder?"

Comparing what you notice about yourself with what others see can give you a fuller picture of how ADHD shows up in your life.

Remember that these boxes aren't permanent labels. Symptoms can shift with stress, sleep, support, or medication. The goal is simply to notice what's true for you right now so you can track patterns, spot changes, and figure out what helps.

HOW ADHD SHOWS UP FOR YOU

1 = Very Often | 2 = Sometimes | 3 = Hardly Ever

1	2	3	**Focus, Memory, and Mental Energy**
☐	☐	☐	I get distracted really easily.
☐	☐	☐	I forget what I'm supposed to do, even right after hearing it.
☐	☐	☐	I lose things like my phone, homework, or headphones a lot.
☐	☐	☐	I start tasks but don't finish them.
☐	☐	☐	I avoid schoolwork or chores that take a lot of brain effort.
☐	☐	☐	I zone out or space out when people are talking.
☐	☐	☐	I have trouble following directions.
☐	☐	☐	I struggle to get organized–like with my backpack, schedule, or room.
☐	☐	☐	I don't turn in assignments even when I've done them.
☐	☐	☐	I feel tired or low on energy a lot, even when I've had sleep.

1	2	3	**Energy, Movement, and Impulses**
☐	☐	☐	I feel like I'm always on the go or can't sit still.
☐	☐	☐	I fidget, pace, or move around even when I'm supposed to sit.

1	2	3	**Energy, Movement, and Impulses**
☐	☐	☐	I talk a lot or interrupt people without meaning to.
☐	☐	☐	I say things or make decisions without thinking them through.
☐	☐	☐	I get too excited or intense sometimes.
☐	☐	☐	I have a hard time calming down once I'm upset or worked up.
☐	☐	☐	I do risky or impulsive things I later regret.

1	2	3	**Emotions, Sensitivity, and Mood**
☐	☐	☐	I get overwhelmed or overreact to small things.
☐	☐	☐	I feel super sensitive–like I take things too personally.
☐	☐	☐	I get upset when things aren't fair.
☐	☐	☐	I feel moody or like my emotions change fast.
☐	☐	☐	I worry a lot about messing up or failing.
☐	☐	☐	I feel anxious or panicky.
☐	☐	☐	I feel insecure or like I'm not good enough.
☐	☐	☐	I feel clingy or need a lot of reassurance.
☐	☐	☐	I expect the worst or assume things will go wrong.
☐	☐	☐	I think people don't like me or are mad at me even if they're not.
☐	☐	☐	I feel sad or down a lot.
☐	☐	☐	I have low self-esteem.
☐	☐	☐	I try to be perfect or get really upset over small mistakes.

1	2	3	**When ADHD Gets in the Way**
☐	☐	☐	My symptoms get in the way of school, friendships, or my home life.
☐	☐	☐	I've noticed I'm struggling more than most people my age.
☐	☐	☐	I want tools to help me manage my emotions, focus, or energy better.

Looking for a way to talk to your parents or doctor about your ADHD symptoms? Use your results from "How ADHD Shows Up for You" to indicate what you're noticing. It can make the conversation easier and more focused.

Yes, Having ADHD Can Be Difficult, But . . .

If you live with ADHD, you already know it can be a lot. The world is designed for people who sit still, lock onto one task until it's done, bounce back from emotions in seconds, and show up five minutes early–basically, the opposite of how your system likes to run.

Once you see how your system really works, you can stop blaming yourself and start building supports that fit. You're not broken. You're learning how you work.

There's no magic wand, but there is knowledge, support, and a toolbox waiting for you. Think of this book as your starter kit. Together, we'll explore, experiment, and discover what works for you.

Ready? Let's go.

2

ADHD, a Raccoon in a Hoodie, and Other Pictures

ADHD can be confusing. One minute you're hyperfocused, finishing a three-hour art project like a creative genius. The next you're wandering the house looking for your phone . . . only to realize it's been in your hand the whole time.

Your brain can feel loud, fast, distracted, brilliant, and frustrating—all at once. It shoves exciting ideas in your face, then drops them halfway through. It pushes you to start something right now, then forgets why it mattered five minutes later. From the outside, it might look like you're keeping it together. But inside, your thoughts zigzag, collide, and race in a hundred directions.

This chapter is about describing your *lived reality* of ADHD—not how it looks to others but how it feels in your own head. Metaphors can help you do this. They help turn hard-to-explain things—like emotions, focus, or memory—into something you can actually picture. The right image can help you see what is happening and start working with it, not against it.

There isn't only one way ADHD feels. In the next few pages, you'll meet three people who created metaphors that made sense of their experience. As you read, notice which parts feel familiar, and start imagining what *your* metaphor might look like.

The Invisible Raccoon

"I have an invisible raccoon living in my brain," Nico said. "Most of the time I don't notice it, but it's always messing with something."

One night, Nico zipped his calculator into the inside pocket of his backpack, proud of himself for being so prepared for a math quiz. But by morning? Disaster. The raccoon had apparently chewed up the memory of where the calculator was. Nico spent forty-five minutes tearing through the house, stress-ranting at his mom (who hadn't even said anything), and stormed out late for class, furious and feeling betrayed by his own brain.

"It's like it knocks over boxes in my head," he explained. "Boxes with memories, plans, what I was supposed to do next. Then it chews on the cords that connect everything. I can't find my headphones, I forgot to charge my phone, and I've opened a second box of cereal when the first one's literally right there."

The raccoon didn't stop at Nico's memory. It clawed at his planning and focus too, leaving him with things like:

- confusing priorities so that cleaning his closet felt more urgent than finishing his lab report

- hitting snooze on starting a task so he ended up scrolling instead
- unplugging his sense of time so five minutes turned into forty-five

When Nico described his ADHD as a raccoon in a green hoodie that lives in his brain and messes with his systems, he separated himself from the symptoms so he could understand what was happening. He wasn't the raccoon; he was the person trying to keep it from tearing open the snack drawer.

Once he named his metaphor—and even laughed about it—he started figuring out what actually works to calm the raccoon down. He's learning what helps: setting reminders, writing things down right away, and creating systems that fit his brain instead of pretending it should work like everyone else's.

The raccoon's still there, but these days, it feels more like a quirky roommate than a housewrecker. Nico still forgets things or freezes when it's time to start. But instead of spiraling into shame, he shrugs and says, "Okay. The raccoon got in again. Not a crisis. I can figure this out."

The Quest for Functioning

Jayden can design a robotic arm, memorize Shakespeare, and win a debate without notes. But brushing his teeth? Packing a backpack? Getting out the door on time? Those feel impossible.

People notice his talent—and they also notice that everyday things trip him up. Most mornings he's racing out the door half dressed, Chromebook forgotten under his bed, and his parents scold him about not handling the "simple stuff."

"I know it shouldn't be this hard," he told me. "I've done way harder things than packing a backpack."

But an ADHD brain doesn't activate for tasks that seem mundane. It craves urgency and interest. Jayden calls this his Mount Doom problem—a reference to *The Lord of the Rings*, where carrying the cursed ring feels exhausting and full of obstacles. Though the quest is exciting, getting there? Not so much. That's how daily life feels for Jayden: Small chores feel like dragons, alarms feel like ambushes, and school mornings feel like marching through lava.

Once he named his metaphor, he created strategies: packing his bag the night before, labeling alarms ("The Orcs Are Coming"), even narrating his morning like a quest. The metaphor gave him a way to explain what was happening inside and a plan to handle it.

The changes didn't happen overnight. Even after he created his mental picture and tried new routines, Jayden got overwhelmed. Gave up. Tried again.

Jayden's Mount Doom shows how ADHD can make everyday tasks feel like quests with no glory. The ADHD brain doesn't shut down because things are hard; it shuts down because they feel pointless. Give it a dragon to slay and it'll rise to the challenge. Ask it to find matching socks and it will collapse.

Mech Suit Mode

Zahra says her ADHD emotions make her feel like she's trapped in a giant mech suit, the kind from action movies or video games. "It's like I'm just living my life, and then—boom—I'm stomping around, knocking stuff over, yelling things I don't even mean. And I don't remember getting into the suit."

One night, her little brother spilled a drink on her open laptop. He apologized right away. But Zahra felt her jaw clench, her neck tighten, and that burning pressure behind her eyes. Before she could stop it, her voice came out too loud.

"Are you serious right now?!" she exploded. Inside, she knew it was too much. But the mech suit had already powered on.

A mech suit is designed to protect, but it also amplifies everything. Even the smallest movement becomes a massive stomp. Inside, Zahra is still herself, but her emotional alarm is blaring so loudly that the part of her brain that usually keeps things in perspective can't keep up. With ADHD, feelings can skip straight past mildly annoyed and rocket to meltdown in seconds.

Realizing this helped Zahra reframe. She's not mean or bad; she's in protective overdrive. Now she's practicing noticing the early signs:

- muscle pain in her neck
- her voice sharpening
- her thoughts flipping into all-or-nothing mode

If she catches the suit powering up, she has a chance to pause and steer. And if she doesn't? She still knows she can step out afterward–apologize, repair, and reset.

Zahra's mech suit shows what it's like when emotions go full throttle.

What's Your Metaphor?

Each of these metaphors–Nico's invisible raccoon, Jayden's Mount Doom, and Zahra's mech suit–offers more than a clever image. They tell the truth about what ADHD feels like from the inside.

Now it's your turn. Use the metaphor flow chart below to help you.

What kind of metaphor feels most like your brain?
Choose the one that feels right—or try more than one

A Character
- What would you name it (e.g., Captain Focus, The Distractorino)?
- What does it look like or wear?
- What does it do that causes trouble?
- Does it ever accidentally help you?
- If you could talk to it, what would you say?

A Place or Scene
- What kind of place matches your ADHD brain (e.g., a cluttered bedroom, a carnival, a *Minecraft* server with no rules)?
- What's going on in that place?
- What's hard? What's oddly fun?

A Feeling or Sensory Mood
- What does it feel like (e.g., a brain full of pop-up ads, static in your chest, sticky thoughts)?
- What object or image matches that feeling?

A Game or Challenge
- What kind of game would it be (e.g., a glitchy level, a laggy multiplayer, a puzzle with missing pieces)?
- Are you the player, the glitch, or both?

Your Metaphor:

____

Your word picture doesn't need to be perfect. It doesn't have to be serious. It just needs to feel true. Some people imagine ADHD as a glitter tornado—brilliant and chaotic. Others picture a group chat where every thought is talking at once, or a *Minecraft* server with no rules and too many players building random stuff at the same time, or a brain where the next thought autoplays before the last one even finished loading. Your metaphor can be weird, messy, dramatic, or oddly specific. If it makes sense to you, that's what matters.

Once you put your experience into words, you gain something powerful: Language. A way to explain it. A way to take it less personally. And eventually, a way to work with it.

What Does Your Metaphor Teach You?

A metaphor isn't simply a clever comparison. It's a shortcut to understanding. The more you return to it, the more clearly

Try It: Create Your ADHD Metaphor

Think of this as giving your experience shape. You can create a character or describe a place, a pattern, or a feeling that captures what ADHD is like for you.

Want to try a character? Use these questions to help:

- *Describe your ADHD metaphor.* (Optional but way more fun. Bonus points for something ridiculous like the Distractorino, Playlist Shuffle Brain, or the Fog Forest.)
- *What does it look like or feel like?* An ogre eating loudly? Glue stuck to your fingers? A maze with no exit signs?
- *What does it do that gets in your way?* Starts five things at once and finishes none? Hijacks your focus midtask? Changes the plan just for the chaos of it?
- *What's one way it accidentally helps you?* Maybe it notices what others miss. Maybe it spins wild ideas that lead somewhere brilliant.
- *If you could talk to it, what would you say?*

you'll see how your system runs—and how you can work with it instead of against it.

Ask yourself:

- What surprised me while I was creating my metaphor?
- How did it help me see ADHD in a new way?
- How might it help someone else understand what I'm going through?
- What strategies or supports could fit this picture?

Your metaphor can grow with you. At first, it might just explain the chaos. Later, it can point toward tools, routines, or even repair strategies that match your brain. The more you practice noticing your metaphor in real life, the less you blame yourself—and the more you know how to steer.

Divergent Thinking Preview

If your metaphor gets weird? Perfect. Permission granted. In chapter 4, we'll dig into divergent thinking—the glistening, outside-the-box way your brain connects ideas.

3

Managing Chaos in the Brain Mansion

Picture your brain as a mansion. A big, busy one with endless rooms, doors, alarms, and random deliveries. Most people have a Butler at the front door—calm and collected, managing the chaos. The Butler keeps track of schedules and belongings. He remembers where you left your water bottle and offers quiet reminders like, *It's time to start math homework* and *Take a breath before you say something you'll regret.* He doesn't panic. He just handles things.

If you have ADHD, though? That Butler might be out back chasing chipmunks, napping, or ghosting his job. Normally, he'd step in to sort things out—deciding what's a real emergency, what's annoying, and how big your reaction should be. But when he's gone, the mansion's Alarm System runs wild.

This Alarm System isn't some sleek, modern setup. It's the screechy school fire alarm kind, with ear-splitting sirens and headache-inducing strobe lights. Even little stuff—like misplacing your phone or being left on read—can set the whole system off, making a small stressor feel like an emergency. Stress takes over, and instead of solving the problem, you might overreact, shut down, or say something you don't mean.

Here's the neuroscience behind the metaphor: The Butler represents your prefrontal cortex—the front part of your brain that helps with planning, focus, and self-management. The Alarm System stands for your limbic system—the emotional center that reacts to stress, danger, and even embarrassment. In many people without ADHD, the Butler and the Alarm System work together: The Butler keeps things calm, and the alarms go off only when they need to. With ADHD,

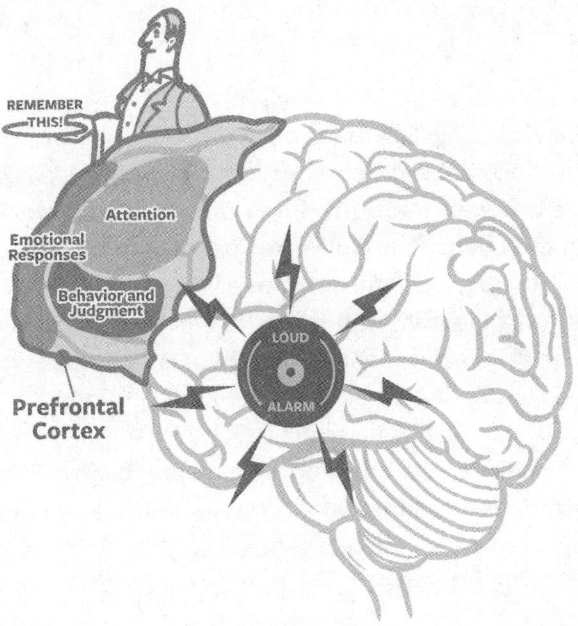

though, the Butler doesn't always show up and the alarms can blast too loud over something small.

Sometimes the Alarm System glitches the other way. It doesn't go off at all. You miss an assignment, run late, or lose something important, and your brain stays weirdly calm—like the alarms didn't notice. Either way, the system is unreliable. Too loud over nothing, silent when it matters. Without the Butler, you're sometimes left swinging between false alarms and radio silence, out of sync with what's really happening.

In this chapter, we'll see what happens when the Butler is offline—how ADHD messes with short-term memory and emotional regulation. We'll look at why your brain sometimes drops the plan or flips into panic mode, and how knowing what's going on helps you handle those moments with more clarity and less shame.

Your Butler and Alarm System

- **Have you ever felt like your Butler was off duty? What was going on?**

- **Now picture your Alarm System. When was the last time the alarms went off?**

Your Alarm System goes off quickly and loudly. Learning when it tends to glitch helps you calm the noise and take back control.

When Your Brain Drops the Whiteboard

In a non-ADHD mansion, the Butler doesn't only greet guests and calm alarms. He carries a whiteboard—a mini board where he jots down everything you're supposed to be doing right now. That whiteboard is your working memory. It holds things like:

- what your professor just said three seconds ago
- what you were about to google before you opened TikTok instead
- the three things your dad told you to grab from the car
- step four of a five-step math problem

When the Butler's paying attention, the whiteboard keeps you on track. But with ADHD, he doesn't always hold it steady. Sometimes he tracks things fine; other times he gets distracted or drops it altogether. And when that happens, planning ahead, following instructions, and staying focused get a lot harder. It's your brain struggling to keep information online—especially when something more interesting, urgent, or emotional hijacks the system—and suddenly you're stuck without the very reminders you need most.

Short-Term Memory vs. Working Memory

Short-term memory is like a sticky note. It holds info for seconds, then it's gone.

Working memory is like the Butler's whiteboard. You're actively using it.

ADHD makes the sticky notes easy to lose and the whiteboard easy to drop.

The Mansion in Meltdown Mode

When the Butler drops the whiteboard, the plan vanishes and the Alarm System takes over. That's why forgetting something small can suddenly feel like a full-blown crisis.

Now picture this: You're already scrambling to remember what you were supposed to do. Then *bam*—someone says something that hits a nerve, or you remember a quiz you didn't study for. Without the Butler steadying things, the Alarm System blares: sirens, flashing lights, all-out emergency mode. Instead of pausing to think, *What are my options?*, your brain jumps straight to panic, shame, or rage. This is called emotional flooding. It's when your feelings crash in before the plan has a chance to load. Emotional flooding can happen anytime—especially if you're already tired, behind, or stressed.

Zahra told me about a morning like this. Running late on four hours of sleep, she suddenly remembered a history quiz. She texted her friend, *Can't meet before class, I need to study.* A moment later, the reply came: *K.*

Her stomach dropped. To her, that single letter felt like proof her friend was mad. With her Butler missing, the alarms screamed, *You messed everything up. Everyone's mad. Fix it. Now.* Her breathing sped up, her face flushed, every sound felt too loud. From the outside, she looked crabby. Inside, she was flooded.

Living at 0 or 10

When your Alarm System glitches, emotions can feel unpredictable—tiny things hit like earthquakes, or big things barely register. One way to make sense of this is by looking at *intensity*. How big does a feeling get? How fast does it take over?

Think of your emotions on a scale from 0 to 10:

0 = flatlined. Zoned out, detached, hard to get moving.

10 = flooded. Maximum intensity. Whatever emotion shows up—anger, panic, excitement, shame—it takes over your whole brain and body.

Most people without ADHD spend a lot of time in the middle of the scale. Feelings build gradually—like annoyance at 3 growing into frustration at 6, but seldom peaking at anger around 9 or 10.

People with ADHD often skip the middle. You can leap straight from 0 to 10 or stay stuck at 0 when you should probably care.

For example:

You're at 0, scrolling YouTube, when your sibling grabs your Rice Krispies Treat without asking. In a flash, you're at 10, shouting like it's the end of the world.

Or you're at 0, zoning out on your phone, when you suddenly remember a project due tomorrow.

Emotional Intensity Scale: What Does It *Feel* Like?

Level	What It Might Feel Like	In Your Brain and Body
0–3: Barely there	*Meh.* You're aware of a feeling, but it's not really affecting you.	You're zoned out, flat, detached. It's hard to care or get going.
4–7: Noticeable but manageable	You know you're feeling something, but you're still in control.	You can think, pause, and respond. It feels like a conversation, not a shout.
8–10: Flooded	You're fully overwhelmed. The emotion takes over everything.	You have a racing heart and tunnel vision. You can't think straight. It feels urgent, even if it's not.

Instead of panicking, you just shrug and keep scrolling, like it barely registers.

Once you can see your range, you're not just along for the ride; you get some say in what happens next.

When Your Brain Glues Feelings to Everything

Here's another curveball ADHD can throw: When the whiteboard drops, the Alarm System tries to make up for it. Instead of holding the fact, it stamps the moment with a feeling—panic, shame, excitement, whatever sticks. It's like your brain saying, "If I can't keep the details, at least you'll remember how it felt."

Ava forgot her notebook. Again. Her lab partners don't yell; they sigh and look away. Tiny moment, right? But inside, Ava feels a gut punch of dread. The Alarm System blares, *This matters. Don't mess it up again.* What her brain holds on to isn't the missing notebook; it's the shame. Now, every time she walks into science class, her shoulders tense. Not because she's remembering the notebook but because that negative feeling has become ingrained in the whole situation.

This is called emotional tagging—a survival strategy your brain uses when working memory drops details. If the whiteboard can't hold the fact, the tag holds the feeling. It's your system trying to protect you, even if it sometimes goes overboard.

Emotional tagging often backfires. When something reminds you of a tagged memory, the feeling rushes in first, even if the situation itself is small. For example:

- A late assignment causes panic—because it carries the weight of the last time you fell behind.

- An unread message stings with shame—because it echoes the time someone left you hanging.
- Asking for help sets off fear—because it recalls the moment you were shut down before.

The new moment feels overwhelming, not because of what's happening right now but because the old emotion is still glued to it.

In this mansion metaphor, ADHD shows up as a Butler who drops the whiteboard, alarms that misfire, and emotions that stick like glue. The systems aren't defective; they're unpredictable. And that unpredictability can make daily life feel harder than it should be.

The more you notice what's happening, the more choices you get. Some days that means calming the alarms; other days it means repairing after an emotional flood. Each step gives you a little more breathing room. You don't have to overhaul the whole mansion at once; you're learning how to care for it room by room.

Memory Glue

Think of a time when a small moment got stuck in your brain—not because it was a big deal but because of how it felt.

- **What happened?**

- **What emotion do you still connect to it—shame, embarrassment, anger, panic?**

- **How has that feeling affected how you act in similar situations now?**

- **How can you change that feeling?**

ADHD brains often tag memories with big feelings. The goal isn't to erase those emotions; it's to notice them. Once you can name what your brain is doing, you have more power to respond instead of reacting.

Reset: What to Do After a Flood

Big feelings hit hard—and fast. But you *can* recover. Here's a reset sequence you can use:

1. *Breathe like you mean it.* Inhale for four seconds, hold for four, exhale for six. Do it three times.
2. *Touch something real.* Hold ice. Run cold water over your hands. Dig your fingers into a hoodie pocket. Anchor your body.
3. *Say what just happened.* "I'm frustrated that . . ." "I'm overwhelmed because . . ."
4. *Move your body.* Shake it out. Walk to the door and back. Stretch. A flooded brain calms faster when your body gets involved. Try dancing to music.
5. *Reboot your Butler.* Ask yourself:
   "What actually needs to happen next?"
   "Can this wait?"
   "Do I need to ask for help?"

You don't have to get it perfect. Try to interrupt the spiral.

4

Like a Squirrel on Espresso Doing Parkour

You sit down to study. You tell yourself, "Okay. No distractions. Just focus on studying for this quiz on mitochondrial function." You think, *Focus. Focus. What's that noise? I think the fridge. Focus. It sounds like my dog is snoring. Did I ever email my professor back? Grandpa doesn't like AI. Did I text him about his birthday? Wait, focus. Mitochondria . . . powerhouse of the cell . . . Oh no. My computer's about to die. I should do laundry. I miss my red alpaca socks. The dog's sleeping on my laundry. She looks like a chicken nugget. Nugget, turkey, gravy. Koala, koala, hamburger.*

Many of my clients describe thought spirals and a constant stream of interesting but not-always-helpful-right-now ideas.

You're not lost; you're just taking the scenic route through a fascinating brain.

Divergent and Convergent Thinking

Your brain has two powerful ways of thinking: divergent and convergent. Everyone uses both, but with ADHD you probably spend more time in divergent mode. That's part of what makes your brain imaginative and original—quick to spot patterns, dream big, and connect dots others might miss.

Divergent thinking is idea mode. It asks "What if?" and spins possibilities in every direction. It doesn't move in a straight line; it branches and leaps, chasing glimmers of interest and curiosity. One idea lights the next . . . and the next . . . until you've covered five topics, six jokes, a Christmas memory, and at least one oddly specific fact about penguins.

Sometimes divergent thinking makes you look brilliant—like when you solve a problem in class in a way no one else even thought of. And sometimes . . . it looks more like a squirrel on espresso doing parkour. One minute you're halfway through your essay, the next you're sketching ideas for a video game, googling ancient Mesopotamian facts, and reorganizing your Spotify playlists.

Convergent thinking is decision mode. Instead of chasing every possibility, it sorts through the options and chooses one to focus on. It's your brain shifting into detective mode—your Sherlock Holmes moment—not to solve a crime but to stay with one topic, make clear choices, and take the next step. Convergent thinking is what helps you decide, commit, and move forward—whether that's finishing a math problem, choosing a thesis statement, or finally unloading the dishwasher.

Here's another way to picture the two types of thinking:

Divergent thinking is the gas pedal—it fuels ideas, possibilities, and momentum.

Convergent thinking is the brake—it helps you slow down, make decisions, and stay in control so you can get somewhere.

Both matter. Press the gas without brakes and it's chaos. Press the brakes without gas and you're stuck in the driveway. You need both pedals to actually drive. With ADHD, your brain probably leans harder on the gas pedal. The skill is learning how to shift between the two so your creativity doesn't blast off but gets you where you want to go.

Your Divergent Thinking Superpowers

Divergent thinking isn't always random distraction. It's one of your superpowers. It's the way your brain creates ideas, notices patterns, and makes connections other people would never think of. Sometimes it feels messy, but underneath the zigzags are real strengths.

You might not see yourself as "creative" in the paint-a-masterpiece or write-a-song sense. But creativity shows up in many forms: asking clever questions, remixing ideas, or solving problems in weird but brilliant ways. Divergent thinking has many sides, and each one can be a strength.

Quick Definitions

Divergent thinking: idea mode. Your brain branches out, asks "What if?," and makes unexpected connections.

Convergent thinking: decision mode. Your brain narrows in, asks "What now?," and helps you follow through to the end.

Curiosity and Fluency: Your Fuel for Ideas

Divergent thinking relies on curiosity and fluency. When both are active, your mind opens wide and ideas start to multiply with ease.

Curiosity is what makes you dig deeper instead of skimming the surface. You don't want the answer; you want to know how it works, why it matters, and what else is connected. That's why someone with ADHD might become a self-taught expert in video game lore, random history facts, or the secret settings behind the school Wi-Fi.

Fluency is the speed of your idea flow. While someone else is still on their first suggestion, you might already have twenty-four. Tyler, a college freshman, groaned about his "too many ideas" problem. "Ack! I could go in so many directions!" he told me about his writing assignment.

Eventually, he realized this wasn't a weakness; it was fuel. He dumped every idea onto paper in five minutes, then

Following the Spark

- What kinds of things spark your curiosity right now?
- When have ideas come so fast you could barely keep up?
- How could you capture that flow before it slips away?

sketched bubble drawings of his top three. His mind map helped him choose, combine, or reshape them. Suddenly fluency wasn't overwhelming; it was a tool.

Curiosity asks the questions. Fluency floods you with possibilities. Together, they mean your brain never runs out of things to think about. It just needs help focusing them.

Flexibility and Elaboration: How You Play with Ideas

Not every idea comes out perfect the first time. Some thoughts require a shift in perspective, while others need further development before they truly shine. That's where flexibility and elaboration come in. They're the parts of divergent thinking that help you *play* with ideas until they actually work.

Flexibility means being able to shift your thinking and see things from another angle. You can look at a situation one way, then flip it around and notice something completely different. That makes you great at collaborating, arguing your point, or coming up with creative fixes when things don't go as planned.

Miriam is the captain of her soccer team. She showed flexible thinking when a sudden downpour made the field too slippery for drills. Instead of canceling practice, she pivoted and took the team under the covered bleachers, leading strategy plays and passing footwork. She didn't get stuck in thinking that they needed a field; she shifted, and her team continued to improve.

Elaboration is what happens when you don't stop at the first draft. You add on, tweak, and make it better. Whether you're revising an essay, layering new details into a drawing, or upgrading the rules of a game you invented, elaboration helps you take an idea further.

Oliver was assigned a simple civil rights movement timeline. He didn't stop at dates. He added photos of leaders,

Playing with Ideas

- When was a time you changed your approach and it worked out better?
- What's something you've built on or revised until it got stronger?
- How do flexibility and elaboration show up in your schoolwork, hobbies, or friendships?

short quotes, QR codes linking to videos, and a "then and now" section connecting history to today. His elaboration made a basic project interactive and memorable.

Flexibility helps you adapt when things change. Elaboration helps you build something stronger out of what you already have. But divergent thinking doesn't stop there. It can also push you into completely new territory when you create something new or when you make surprising connections that make people laugh.

Originality and Humor: Fresh Takes and Quick Wit

Originality and humor often travel together. Both come from your brain making quick, unexpected leaps. Sometimes those leaps land as a bold new idea, other times as a perfectly timed joke.

Originality shows up when you don't just follow the template; you remix it. You rethink and twist things until they feel fresh.

Charlotte skipped the usual flower-and-sunset photos for a nature photo contest. Instead, she shot raindrops clinging to a basketball net, each drop reflecting the court behind it.

Spot Your Fresh Takes and Quick Wit

Think about a time when your originality or humor showed up. Write a few quick notes:

- **What was the situation?**
- **What did you say, create, or do that felt different?**
- **How did people react to what you said or did, or how did the moment shift for you?**
- **What does that tell you about how your brain works?**

Originality and humor don't always look big. They can be tiny twists or quick quips. But each one is proof that your mind sees the world from a unique angle.

Humor works the same way—it's originality delivered at just the right moment.

When asked to define "endothermic reaction," Sam shrugged and said, "Basically like me trying to get out of bed—it always takes extra energy."

The teacher raised an eyebrow, then nodded and said, "Accurate—and oddly . . . well put." Humor works by flipping a situation with a surprising link—a quick mental leap that others didn't see coming.

Both originality and humor reframe the world so people see it differently. Sometimes that means creating something striking and new. Other times it means making people laugh. Either way, you're showing a perspective only you can bring.

Divergent thinking is one of your brain's best tools. It opens doors to new possibilities, unexpected connections, and ideas that grow bigger than you imagined. When you balance it with focus and follow-through, it can lead to innovative solutions and exciting projects. The key is knowing when to keep generating ideas and when to choose a direction and run with it.

Divergent Thinking	**Convergent Thinking**
Brainstorming wild ideas for your group project	Deciding which one you'll do
Writing three intro paragraphs for your essay	Choosing one paragraph and finishing the draft
Imagining six different ways your friend *might* be mad at you	Texting them to ask *if* they're mad at you
Creating a list of Halloween costume ideas, with props, lighting, and backstories	Picking one costume and finding pants that match

What are your divergent thinking superpowers? Write them down. Tell someone who knows you about them. Own them.

When Divergent Thinking Takes Over

Your brain's idea mode is amazing—until it runs nonstop. Instead of moving projects forward, it floods you with too many options and not enough follow-through.

Here are six common ways ADHD brains have trouble shifting out of divergent mode.

Being Stuck in Brainstorm Mode

You sit down to start your art presentation. Ten minutes in, you've got three topics. Thirty minutes in, you've got eight more. By midnight, you've researched three, switched topics twice, and invented a side project you're not turning in. What you don't have is a finished presentation.

That's the brainstorm trap—idea after idea, none of them landing. Your brain is chasing possibilities like a golden retriever with a bucket of tennis balls. It's excited but not actually getting anywhere.

What helps is putting a boundary around brainstorming. Give yourself a window—maybe twenty minutes—where your only job is to let the ideas fly. When the timer goes off, it's time to choose. Narrow it down, commit, and move forward. You're not shutting down creativity. You're steering it into something real.

Dodging the Easy Stuff

Sometimes the problem isn't that a task is too hard. It's that it feels too easy.

Spotting the Brainstorm Trap

Think about the last time you kept generating ideas but didn't finish.

- **What were you working on?**

- **How many different ideas did you come up with?**

- **Did you ever decide on one, or did it stall out?**

- **What could help you set a "decide by" moment next time?**

For his recital, Mario was asked to start with Canon in D, a beginner piece almost every piano student learns. But because he found it boring, he barely practiced it. When it came time to perform, his lack of preparation showed. He stumbled through notes, restarted, and couldn't keep momentum. It felt less like a performance and more like a rehearsal gone wrong.

The work-around is to give your brain a reason to care. For Mario, that might mean turning the simple Canon in D into a challenge, like playing it flawlessly three times in a row. Or

Making the Boring Stuff Work

Think of a time something felt too easy, so you didn't give it your best.

- **What happened when it was time to do it?**

- **How could you have gamified it, paired it with a reward, or set a microgoal?**

- **Which strategy do you want to try the next time you hit an "ugh, this is boring" moment?**

he could pair it with something he does enjoy, like practicing the dull piece once, then rewarding himself by running through an experimental one. He could even set a microgoal, like making the "easy" song sound as smooth and expressive as possible, almost like a concert pianist showing off.

You don't have to love the basics. You just need to make them interesting enough that your brain stays engaged.

Having Big Ideas but No Follow-Through

"I'm the creative one," Sasha told me. "I come up with the cool stuff. Everyone else can figure out the rest."

As president of her school's theater club, Sasha had bold, exciting ideas for posters, events, and campaigns. Her vision lit up the room and made people want to join in.

But she struggled with the follow-through. She didn't answer group texts, showed up late to meetings, and forgot to book the rehearsal space—twice. Frustration grew, members stopped showing up, and what once felt inspiring began to feel chaotic.

Sasha thrived on the divergent side of leadership—the brainstorming and thrill of imagining what could be. But she avoided the convergent side—the steady steps and unglamorous details that turn an idea into something real. She

From Spark to Follow-Through

Think of one big idea you had that lost steam.

- **What made the idea exciting at first?**

- **What details got dropped or avoided?**

- **Who or what could help you anchor the follow-through (a reminder, a partner, a checklist)?**

- **How would it feel if that idea landed instead of just floating?**

eventually realized that vision alone wasn't enough. Without structure, even the best ideas fizzle.

If you fall in love with your divergent ideas, you don't have to stop being the big-picture person. Sasha learned that she needed support so the details didn't slip through. She set reminders, asked a friend to provide accountability, and divided up responsibilities so details didn't get dropped.

Big ideas matter—but they only change the world if someone makes sure the lights are on when the curtain rises.

Facing the Pressure of Potential

Juan was the kid who made everything look easy. He was smart, funny, and overflowing with ideas. Everyone expected something amazing from him. For a while, he expected it of himself too.

By the time he hit college, those expectations no longer felt exciting. They felt heavy. "Potential" wasn't just praise anymore; it was pressure. Everyone seemed to be waiting for Juan to do something remarkable, but he had no idea what that "something" was.

He was good at chemistry and biology, so maybe medicine was the path. But he also loved writing, so journalism sounded exciting. Then again, he'd daydream about running his own import business . . . until a friend joked he should try stand-up, and suddenly comedy felt possible too. Each option led to another, and instead of choosing, he kept circling. The more paths he pictured, the harder it was to take a single step.

When you have ADHD, you often have a powerful imagination—one of your greatest strengths—and sometimes it works against you. You can picture every scenario of what you could do with your life, but instead of choosing, you stall out.

From Potential to Progress

Think of a time when the words "you have potential" felt like pressure.

- **What goal or future were you imagining?**

- **Did the pressure help you move, or did it freeze you?**

- **What's one small, real step you could take today because it matters to you?**

Juan eventually realized that chasing a flawless future wasn't helping. Instead, he picked one small goal that mattered to him, not to impress anyone else. Then he broke it down into steps:

What would this look like in real life?
What's the first action I can take?
What could get in the way, and how do I plan for it?

Once he shifted from "What if?" to "What's next?," the pressure started to ease. His imagination didn't disappear; it stopped running the show.

Spiraling into What-Ifs

Your brain is extraordinary at imagining possibilities. That's one of its superpowers. But when worry takes over, that same talent can turn into a doomscroll of what-ifs.

It often starts small. *What if I fail this test?* Then it multiplies. *What if I fail the class? What if I don't graduate? What if I never get into college or find a job or have a life or . . .*

Noah got a 72 percent on a science test. To him, that was a disaster. By the next morning, he'd convinced himself his

Flipping What-Ifs into Action

Think about the last time your brain spiraled into what-ifs.

- What started the spiral?

- Which worries were real, and which were false alarms?

- What's one small action you could have taken instead of worrying?

- How can you remind yourself next time that worrying isn't the same as solving?

GPA was ruined, no college would accept him, and he'd be stuck at home forever—all because of one grade.

That's how quickly ADHD plus anxiety can turn one bump into a full-on avalanche. Your imagination spins out disaster after disaster, each one louder than the last. The trap is that it feels like preparation, but it isn't. You're not getting safer; you're just getting stuck.

The way out is shifting from problem-finding to problem-solving. Ask yourself, *If this is a real issue, what's the very next step I can take? If it's only a scary story my brain made up, can I call it what it is—a false alarm—and let it go?*

Noah eventually learned to pause when the spiral started. Instead of chasing every disaster, he asked, *What can I actually do today?* Sometimes that meant studying a little extra. Other times it meant reminding himself, *This is just one test. It won't matter to the overall picture.*

Overcomplicating Everything

You've probably seen those TikToks or YouTube shorts where a marble rolls down a track, knocks over dominoes, launches a lever, pops a balloon, and finally flips a pancake. That's a Rube Goldberg machine—something ridiculously complicated doing something super simple.

ADHD brains sometimes build those machines out of everyday tasks. What should be one step turns into a whole chain of "must do first" jobs.

Lily wanted to clean her desk. Simple enough. But then she thought, *I should reorganize the drawers so it stays clean.* That meant dumping everything onto the surface. Next, she figured she should dust before putting stuff back, but the microfiber cloth was in the laundry. In order to do laundry, she had to grab the basket from the car. The basket still had her hockey gear inside.

An hour later, her desk was messier than before, her gear was scattered across the floor, and she was curled up watching videos of people making tiny clay food. Lily had created a Rube Goldberg machine—when one step multiplies into ten and slows down or prevents you from completing the task.

The way forward is to pause and ask yourself, *What's the real task here?* For Lily, it wasn't "reorganize the whole system"; it was simply "tidy the desk." Once you've named the job, shrink it into simple moves: Pick up the books, wipe the surface, throw away the trash. You don't have to solve everything before you begin.

Cutting Out the Extra Steps

Think about the last time one small job turned into ten.

- What was the original task?
- How many "must do firsts" did you add?
- What could the one actual step have been?
- How might it have felt to finish the real job without all the extras?

When you cut out the extra steps, you don't create the complicated mechanisms.

Learning to Shift Your Thinking

One of the hardest parts of managing an ADHD brain is knowing when to switch gears. Stay in idea mode too long and nothing gets finished. Stay in decision mode too long and you shut down new possibilities. Try to do both at once, and it's like pressing the gas and brake together—you burn energy but don't actually move.

Marcus, who edits videos for his YouTube channel, used to struggle with this. Brainstorming ideas? Divergent mode. Trimming clips and syncing transitions? Convergent mode. When he tried to brainstorm and finalize at the same time, his editing slowed to a crawl. Either the ideas spun forever, or he cut them off before they had a chance to grow. Over time, Marcus noticed the pattern. He stopped trying to do both at once. Now he gives himself space to brainstorm first—messy notes, half-formed ideas, no pressure to decide. Later, he switches gears and edits with a different mindset. The work moves faster and the videos end up stronger because each mode gets its own turn.

Divergent thinking gives you ideas. Convergent thinking provides the focus and structure to carry them out. Both are valuable, but the real skill is learning when to lean on each one.

All those strengths you read about—curiosity, fluency, flexibility, elaboration, originality, and humor—work best when you can shift modes on purpose. Let your ideas run wild when you're in idea mode, then, when it's time to act, focus in, make choices, and move forward.

That's how you turn "What if?" into "What's next?"

Spot It, Shift It, Do It

Think of something you worked on this week.

- Were you in idea mode (divergent thinking) or decision mode (convergent thinking)?
- How did staying in that mode help you or trip you up?
- What sign tells you it's time to switch?
- What's one thing you can try to practice shifting on purpose?

5

Real Power-Ups vs. Fake Power-Ups

Have you noticed how your motivation comes in random bursts—like one day you're unstoppable, and the next you can't even start a two-minute task?

Or how you can get lost in a game, show, or project for hours, but totally stall on a simple assignment?

Or how the only time you finally get moving is when the deadline is in your face?

When you have ADHD, motivation can feel like a mystery. That unpredictability is a sign that your brain is running on a different operating system.

ADHD isn't only about attention; it's also about interest and motivation. Dr. Russell Barkley, an ADHD expert, explains that it's not that you can't pay attention; it's that your brain's "start button" is picky about when it works.* That button is usually triggered by two things: when something grabs your attention, and how strongly you feel about it.

- *Your "why."* Your brain needs a reason that feels personal before it kicks into gear. Curiosity, excitement, urgency, or genuine importance—without that "why," getting started feels almost impossible.
- *Big emotions.* Feelings drive your motivation. With ADHD, emotions hit hard and fast. A small win can make you soar; a minor setback can knock you flat. Those surges don't only change your mood; they also fuel your drive.

Put those together, and ADHD motivation makes more sense. When curiosity or urgency lights up, you're all in. But when something feels boring or routine, your brain hunts for shortcuts—stress, anger, shame, or distraction—to push the button. Those shortcuts work like fake power-ups. They give you a jolt in the moment but drain your energy and leave you stuck again.

In this chapter, we'll look at the fake power-ups the ADHD brain reaches for when progress stalls—and then explore real power-ups that actually help you advance without burning out.

Dodging Moves

Sometimes the easiest way to handle a hard task is . . . not to. ADHD brains are experts at dodging by diving into side quests. These dodges feel like they're helping in the

* Russell A. Barkley, *Taking Charge of ADHD: The Complete, Authoritative Guide for Parents*, 4th ed. (Guilford Press, 2022).

moment, but they're fake power-ups that drain your energy and leave you scrambling later.

Avoidance

Claudia had a huge project due. Instead of opening her laptop, she decided her room absolutely needed a new photo wall. She spent the afternoon scrolling Pinterest, printing pics at Walgreens, and staying up way too late arranging them around her LED lights. "At least my room looks amazing," she said. Her wall looked great, but the project was still untouched.

ADHD brains are good at chasing "urgent" side quests—color-coding notes, reorganizing a closet, redesigning a playlist, or recording a TikTok. Each one feels satisfying, but it's a fake power-up.

AVOIDANCE SELF-CHECK

Think of the "real task" as the thing you're supposed to be doing. The "decoy task" is the thing you're doing instead.

- ☐ Am I doing a decoy task to avoid the real task?
- ☐ Does the decoy task feel urgent even though the real task matters more?
- ☐ Did I pick the decoy task because it's easier or more comfortable than the real task?
- ☐ Am I ignoring or downplaying the consequences of not doing the real task?
- ☐ Have I already told myself "I'll do the real task later" more than once?

If most of your answers are "yep," you're probably in avoidance mode. The next step isn't beating yourself up; it's noticing the avoidance, naming it, and deciding whether to shift back to the real task.

Avoidance shows up when the work feels tedious, overwhelming, or risky. Your brain whispers, "Do anything else," and suddenly the side quest feels like the main quest.

Together, Claudia and I made a list of questions she can ask herself when avoidance takes over.

Why did I think this task was important?

Is there a deadline?

What happens if I don't finish it?

Have I set aside time to do it?

"Usually, my brain whines back, 'But I don't want to!'" Claudia said. And that's the giveaway. It's not about time management; it's about facing avoidance head-on.

If you're not dodging with side quests, you might be bogged down waiting for panic to show up. That's where procrastination kicks in.

Procrastination

Avoidance and procrastination can look the same, but they are not. Avoidance is swapping the real task for another that feels easier or more fun. Procrastination is waiting until panic or perfection finally forces you to move.

Everybody puts things off sometimes, but for many of us with ADHD, procrastination is the go-to. It usually starts with a thought like, *I don't feel like doing that right now.* We picture some magical future moment when we'll suddenly want to do it. And then . . . we wait.

Evan, a senior, laughed as he told me, "My English paper was assigned in September."

Oh no. It's November, I thought.

"I started it last night. Wrote twelve pages in one sitting. Finished five minutes before the bell." He grinned like he'd beaten the system.

That last-minute rush can feel powerful, like a buzzer-beater shot. The problem is that it's a fake power-up. Evan used procrastination to give him a sense of urgency, which gave him a jolt of adrenaline. Research shows we don't actually work better under pressure. We make more mistakes, work less creatively, and remember less of what we did. The thrill is our nervous system in overdrive, not a productivity hack.

If you are waiting for the "right mood" to start a project, call it what it really is—procrastination. Then you can find more effective ways to create urgency:

- Create a mini race. Set a fake deadline a few hours or days earlier.
- Shrink the start. Break it into a five-minute action.
- Borrow momentum. Work alongside a friend or join a body-doubling session.
- Use music, a short walk, or a hype text to get moving before panic takes over.

Procrastination's Twin: Perfectionism

Sometimes procrastination isn't about waiting for panic; it's about holding out for that impossible moment when you finally feel "ready enough" to be certain you won't fail. That's the perfectionist version of procrastination.

Procrastination Red Flags

"I'll do it later" keeps sliding down the calendar.

You're hoping motivation will just show up.

You rely on last-minute panic to get started.

Maya loved creative writing, but when her teacher assigned a short story, she didn't do anything for weeks. In her head, she imagined her classmates judging every word. If it couldn't be guaranteed amazing, it felt safer not to start.

Many of my clients find themselves in this loop. They care a lot about the task. They picture their failure before they even begin. They avoid starting it. They panic at the last minute and rush to complete it. And then they beat themselves up and repeat the process.

Perfectionistic procrastination feels like protection, but it is really just another false power-up. It prevents you from risking imperfection, which also stops you from starting. But you don't have to lower your standards. You just need different tools to get there:

- Limit your edits. Give yourself one draft and one round of fixes, then hit submit.
- Get feedback early. Share a rough version with a teacher, coach, or friend before you sink hours into polishing. An outside perspective is way more useful than spiraling in your head.

Procrastination will still show up sometimes, but you can start the "race" earlier and with less pressure. That way, you get the focus without the crash that comes from running only on fake power-ups.

The Pressure Pushes

Sometimes the only way ADHD brains get moving is through pressure. Stress, urgency, or frustration can feel like jet fuel in the moment. These pressure pushes act like fake power-ups: They light a fire under you, but the boost doesn't last and the crash can hit hard.

Anxiety: Running on Urgency

When deciding what to do feels impossible, anxiety can take over—and that surge of nervous energy is often what finally gets you moving. You scramble to start at the last minute, not because the task suddenly becomes easier but because the pressure feels unbearable. *After all*, you reason, *if something makes me panicky, it must be important, right?*

That's what Liam does. A week before his project check-in, his brain starts pacing. *What if I forget to turn it in? What if I mess it up? What if my teacher doesn't like what I've done?* The more he worries, the more "motivated" he feels.

Zoe uses anxiety for smaller stuff. She had to bring snacks for her field hockey party. A simple reminder—*Don't forget the snacks*—swirled into *What if there's not enough? What if people hate them?* She checked the bag three times on the way there, even though the snacks were fine.

Then there's Quinton, who always arrives early. If he has to be somewhere at 4:00, he shows up at 3:40, heart pounding. "I don't even know why," he said. "I just can't handle the feeling of maybe being late." He calls it being prepared, but he's running on anxiety fuel.

Anxiety can feel useful, but when it's your main fuel, it burns through your energy. And it often spills onto the people around you because you are more likely to rant, snap, or vent your stress until everyone else is also tense. When the pressure of the stress gets too high, you often stall out instead of finishing.

A better move is to notice when you're leaning on anxiety and swap to calmer strategies. Here are a few reset steps you can take when you're running on anxiety:

- Take one slow breath—in for four seconds, hold for four, out for six.
- Check your body. Relax your jaw, shoulders, or bouncing leg.
- Name it: "I'm running on anxiety fuel."
- Anchor your focus with a timer, playlist, or study buddy.
- Replace panic with curiosity. Ask yourself, "What's one tiny thing I could try?"

Urgency can be effective in short bursts, but it isn't a sustainable long-term strategy.

Maybe you don't rely on anxiety. Do you use anger instead?

Anger: Mad Fuel

Sometimes frustration motivates you into action.

Mateo had been putting off tuning his bike. Then his brother left it in the rain, and the chain rusted. "Seriously?!" Mateo yelled. He spent two hours scrubbing, oiling, and adjusting until it worked perfectly. His anger propelled him into action.

Harper did the same with dishes piling up in her room. Her dad walked in and said, "Your room smells like a science experiment." She bolted up, stomped into the kitchen, and scrubbed every plate while muttering that it did not smell like a science experiment.

Zane's trigger happened during practice. His coach teased, "Guess some people don't care about making the lineup." Zane went home feeling angry and insulted, drilled for three hours, and played harder than ever the next day.

Anger is another fake power-up. It provides a strong rush of energy, but that energy burns out quickly and often causes you to snap at people who don't deserve it. Even though it can get you moving when nothing else does, it's not a fuel you can rely on. Once the flare passes, you'll need real power-ups to keep going. If you catch yourself using mad fuel:

- Knock out the one thing you're fired up about, then stop.
- Let the anger go instead of replaying it.
- Aim it at the task, not the people around you.
- Shift into calmer motivation before the spark fizzles.

When anger fizzles out, something heavier often slips in. That's when shame takes over.

Shame: The Self-Attack Trap

Shame doesn't flare up and fade like anger. It sticks around, clinging to you like damp clothes after a rainstorm. For many with ADHD, when avoidance, procrastination, anxiety, and anger lose their energy, shame quietly takes their place.

Guilt and shame aren't the same. Guilt says, "I messed up." Shame says, "I *am* the mess-up." Guilt points to an action you can repair. Shame attacks who you are.

After enough moments of messing up, you start calling yourself out before anyone else does. You hear the criticism in your head before anyone else speaks because you already know what they'll say. Over time, the outside voices become your inner voice.

That's where Livvie was stuck. She wasn't just mad about missing a deadline; she was mad at herself. "I can't get my life together," she told me. "I'm a failure. I'm tired of being me." That's what shame does. It stops being about the homework or the deadline and turns into a story about who you are.

Shame is another fake power-up. It might push you to act, but it does so by tearing you down. The cost is huge—drained energy, harsh self-talk, and the belief that you're not enough.

What helps instead is choosing curiosity and connection over cruelty. When you find shame creeping in, try these things instead:

- Talk it out with someone who sees the bigger picture—a parent, teacher, coach, or trusted friend.
- Connect with someone before you try to push through. A quick text or call can break shame's grip.
- Start tiny. Pick one step so small it feels almost silly.
- Ask, "What's making this hard?" instead of "Why am I like this?"

Shame will try to convince you that you don't deserve kindness or support. That's exactly when you need both the most.

All these traps—avoidance, procrastination, perfectionism, anxiety, anger, and shame—can get you moving. That's why your brain keeps reaching for them. But they are fake power-ups. They give you a quick rush, then leave you drained, stressed, or doubting yourself.

The good news is you don't have to run on fake power-ups forever. There are real power-ups you can use instead—strategies that increase your motivation without burning you out. They may not feel as dramatic in the moment, but they build steady momentum and make it easier to trust yourself over time. That shift doesn't happen overnight. But the more you practice, the easier it gets to swap a fake power-up for a real one.

Real Power-Ups: Motivation That Lasts

Fake power-ups work like energy drinks for your brain. They give you a fast spike, then drop you flat. Real power-ups feel different. They may start smaller, but they last—and they help you keep moving without draining your energy or wrecking your confidence.

Real power-ups come from things ADHD brains naturally respond to: curiosity, small wins, connection, and support from Future You. Each one gives you inspiration that lasts. Instead of waiting for panic or beating yourself up, you can use these reliable boosts to get started and keep going.

In the next few pages, you'll see what real power-ups look like and how to use them. Try a few and notice which ones click for you. Every time you swap out a fake power-up for a real one, you're training your brain to work with you instead of against you.

Curiosity Sparks

Curiosity may not feel as dramatic as panic or anger, but it can be just as powerful. When your brain is interested, it naturally pays attention. Even a tiny flicker of "what if" can shift you from frozen to moving. Instead of waiting for pressure, try asking yourself one curiosity question:

If I did want to do this task, what would be a good reason to do it?
How could I make this a little more interesting?
What part of this do I care about?

Jayden hated math homework, but when he asked himself, *What's one thing I could figure out without looking at the answer key?*, he ended up finishing half the worksheet before noticing the time.

Sometimes that one question can help you open the doc, make a list, or sketch a first idea, or it might even be enough to get the task done. That little step matters—it's momentum that doesn't rely on fake power-ups.

Mini Wins

Big tasks can feel impossible when we look at them all at once. That's why ADHD brains freeze—we see the whole mountain instead of the first step.

A mini win is the smallest possible action you can take. It could be checking the rubric, writing one slide, or grabbing your notebook. Once you start, your brain receives a small hit of achievement, which may give you momentum for the next step.

Lucia told herself she only had to open the doc and write one sentence. Twenty minutes later, she had three paragraphs done. That one microstep flipped the switch.

Try these mini-win strategies:

- Break the task into one five-minute move.
- Make a "just enough" list so you know when you can stop.
- Celebrate each step instead of waiting until the very end.

Mini wins feel small, but they add up. And unlike fake power-ups, they don't crash. They steady you so the next move is always a little easier.

Body Doubling and Borrowed Energy

Sometimes the hardest part of getting started is feeling alone with the task. ADHD brains often do better when someone else is there—not to do the work for us but to share the space. That's called body doubling.

Kai needed to get some work done, so he chose a two-hour "study with me" video. By the end, he'd finished his outline and texted me: *Why was that easier with strangers on YouTube than by myself in my room?* Watching someone else focus gave his brain an anchor, and suddenly the work didn't feel so heavy. That's the power of body doubling, and there are lots of ways to do it:

- Ask a friend to be your body double while both of you study, even if you're on mute.
- Join an online coworking session or stream a "study with me" video.
- Text someone: *I'm starting now. Check in with me in thirty minutes.*

The point isn't accountability in a strict sense; it's connection. When you borrow momentum from someone else, your brain feels supported instead of stuck.

Teaming Up with Future You

One of the best ways to boost motivation is to stop treating Future You like the dumping ground for all your problems. Flip the script: Let Present You do small things now so Future You feels supported instead of stressed.

Nia explained it this way: "I used to be mad at Past Me for leaving a mess, and Future Me always paid the price. What finally worked was imagining Present Me making things easier. I'd picture Future Me waking up in my bed, and I wanted her to have a good morning. So now I ask Future Me, 'What would help you?' The answers are obvious–pack my bag, pick an outfit, put my phone across the room so I don't scroll until 1:00 a.m." Nia saw better mornings when she had this imaginary conversation.

Ivan used the same trick on his weekly programming assignments that are due on Tuesday morning. "I always want to start them on Saturday," he admitted, "but then I wait until Monday night."

I asked, "What does Friday Ivan need to do for Saturday Ivan?"

He realized he could skim the directions and jot down a few questions on Friday to help him get started on Saturday. The next week, when he came to our coaching session, he explained how thinking about different versions of himself helped him complete the assignment by Monday.

Frannie added her own twist. "One time I was dreading completing my slides," she said. "But when I opened them, Past Me had already dropped in the headings and half the research links. I literally whispered, 'You're a legend.'"

Her friend looked at her. "Wait . . . are you talking to yourself?"

Frannie laughed. "Yep. Past Me crushed it."

It might sound silly, but it works. When you see Future You as a teammate instead of a stranger, procrastination turns into collaboration. You swap guilt for gratitude.

Fake power-ups will always be tempting. They feel fast and familiar, and sometimes they even get you through in the moment. But they drain your energy and leave you stuck in the same loop.

Real power-ups–curiosity sparks, mini wins, body doubling, and teaming up with Future You–are quieter but stronger. Every time you trade a fake power-up for a real

Quick Questions for Future You

Imagine that you are talking to Future You:

- If you could send me a text right now, what would you say?
- What's one thing I can do tonight so tomorrow is easier?
- Will you be glad I stayed up doing this or wish I'd gone to bed?
- If I don't do this now, what will you have to deal with?
- What would make you proud of me in the morning?

Every time you help Future You, you're building a real power-up. It doesn't just move you forward; it reminds you that you can care for yourself in the present and in the future.

one, you're proving to yourself that your motivation doesn't have to come from panic, anger, or shame.

You don't need to fix everything at once. Pick one real power-up and practice it this week. Notice how it feels different. With each step, you're not only getting things done; you're building a story about yourself that's hopeful, steady, and true.

From Fake Power-Ups to Real Ones

Fake Power-Ups Drain Your Battery

Avoidance feels productive, but side quests stall the real work.

Procrastination waits for panic or perfection to push you.

Anxiety is stress-fueled urgency that burns you out.

Anger is a quick jolt that fizzles fast.

Shame pushes you through self-criticism and drains your confidence.

Real Power-Ups Steady Momentum

Curiosity sparks ask one small "what if" question.

Mini wins shrink the mountain into five-minute steps.

Body doubling borrows momentum from someone else.

Teaming up with Future You trades guilt for gratitude.

6

Hidden Forces and Plot Twists: Changing Your Motivation

Motivation with ADHD is full of plot twists. One moment you're ready to go, the next your brain skips the scene altogether. Four hidden forces drive these twists: time blindness, perception of interest, emotional intensity, and energy math.

- *Time blindness:* when "now" feels like all that exists . . . until "later" suddenly crashes in.
- *Perception of interest:* your brain's priority system; exciting things cut to the front, and boring ones disappear off the map.
- *Emotional intensity:* the rocket fuel; big feelings grab control, and low ones let you drift.
- *Energy math:* when your brain guesses your fuel tank by vibe, not reality.

Left on autopilot, these forces can quietly steer you off course before you even realize it. But once you recognize their patterns, you can start steering instead of drifting. Time blindness is the trickiest of the bunch.

Force 1: Time Blindness (Glitching Through Time)

ADHD brains don't feel time the way others do. It's not a steady stream—it's more like glitching frames in a movie. One moment you're in the scene, the next it's gone. Think Miles Morales in *Spider-Verse*—grounded one second, yanked into another dimension the next.

Here's what time glitches can look like:

Time shrink: Jordan figures he has plenty of time before soccer, but suddenly the car horn honks outside.

Time stretch: Harper swears unloading the dishwasher will take forever, but four minutes later, it's done.

Time slip: Riya plays a new game at 10:00 p.m. for a little while, but suddenly it's 2:00 a.m.

The Now/Not-Now Time Bar

ADHD time doesn't feel like a smooth line. It feels like two blocks: now and not-now.

Now is urgent, alive, and real. **Not-now** is vague, far away, almost fake.

Almost everything lives in not-now . . . until it suddenly flips into now.

Tip: Use timers, calendars, or reminders to stretch the time bar so you can see what's coming instead of being ambushed.

Time glitches are real, but so are the ways to manage them. Which ones do you notice most in your own life?

Time isn't the only thing at play. ADHD also runs everything through another filter: *Is this interesting?* That's where the fun factor comes in.

Force 2: Perception of Interest (The Fun Factor)

If ADHD came with a default setting, it would be "Is this fun?" Not "Is this important?" or "Will this help later?" Just "Is this fun right now?"

For ADHD brains, that filter runs everything. The interesting-right-now task takes center stage, while everything else gets shoved to the back. That's why Mateo spends an hour lining up sneakers instead of doing homework, Harper edits videos long past midnight, and Leo finally vacuums once he turns it into a race.

Everyone enjoys fun, but people without ADHD can often push through boring tasks just because they're "supposed to." With ADHD, you need a hook–something that makes the start feel worthwhile.

Why Fun Wins First Place

When you live with ADHD, tasks aren't ranked by importance; they're ranked by spark.

If something feels fun, new, or rewarding, your attention locks in.

If it feels boring, it fades into the background–often until the last minute.

The secret: You don't have to turn boring tasks into something epic. You just need one hook–a timer race, music, or a small reward–that makes it worth starting.

But it isn't always about fun. Sometimes big feelings can steal motivation just as fast as novelty can.

Force 3: Emotional Intensity (The Rocket Fuel Factor)

When you have ADHD, big feelings *are* motivation. They work like rocket fuel: The stronger the surge, the faster you move. Excitement can lock you into hours of focus, while fear can shove you into action at the very last minute.

For Mateo, joy fuels motivation. When creative energy hits, he'll paint for hours and barely notice the time.

For Riya, frustration is the trigger. One sharp comment from her mom about her messy room and suddenly she's reorganizing at full speed, clothes flying everywhere.

Kiya has written papers with both strong positive and negative emotions motivating her. When curiosity takes over, she cranks out her English paper in one focused burst. Other times, it's panic that launches her—heart pounding at 11:58 p.m.—as she races to finish before the deadline.

The stronger the surge, whether it's curiosity, joy, panic, or frustration, the harder it pushes you.

Rocket Fuel Feelings

Big feelings can give you instant focus.

Excitement, curiosity, or joy can launch you into flow.

Panic, fear, or frustration can also launch you—but usually at the last minute.

Here's the catch: Rocket fuel burns out fast.

Tip: Let emotions help you take off, but use simple habits to stay in orbit and finish the mission.

Emotions aren't the only force at play. Even before you start, your brain is making calculations about effort—and it often gets those wrong. That's broken energy math.

Force 4: Energy Math (And Why ADHD Brains Get It Wrong)

ADHD brains do energy math before we even start a task—but the math is usually wrong.

It's like guessing how fast your phone battery will drain. If something feels boring, your brain acts like it'll eat up 80 percent of your charge, even if it's a five-minute job. If it feels exciting, you assume it's barely using power, until the red battery icon flashes at you out of nowhere.

We're not great at reading our own battery gauge. Here's what those glitches look like in real life:

Overestimating the drain: Harper kept putting off folding laundry, convinced it would swallow her whole evening. When she finally started it, it was over in seven minutes.

Underestimating the drain: Mateo spent all afternoon with friends, convinced, *I'm not even tired.* But the second he sat in the car, his tank crashed from full to flashing red.

Misjudging the drain: Jayden put off his history outline, sure it would wear him out. But when he finally started, it was done in under an hour—while the "easy" science questions ended up taking a lot of thinking energy.

Energy math malfunctions can throw you off on their own, but when they combine with time blindness, the effect doubles. Time blindness makes hours disappear until it's

Bad Energy Math in Action

ADHD brains misread the effort gauge.

Overestimate: "This will take forever"—but it's done in fifteen minutes.

Underestimate: "This won't drain me"—but you crash after.

Misjudge: "The easy part will be quick"—surprise, it's the hardest.

Tip: Test your brain's math. Start a timer and try the first step. Reality often beats the guess.

suddenly "later" and you don't know where the time went. Bad energy math makes you misjudge effort—either bracing for exhaustion that never comes or missing the crash until it blindsides you. Together, they convince you that you don't have the time *or* the energy to even start.

Time glitches, the fun factor, rocket fuel feelings, and energy math all bend the plot of your day. The challenge is figuring out which one is blocking you.

That's where the Solve-It Grid comes into play. It highlights two of the strongest forces behind motivation: the fun factor and the rocket fuel factor. In the next chapter, we'll walk through the Solve-It Grid one piece at a time, giving you a clear path to shift out of stuck mode and start making real progress.

7

The Energy Grid

"My brain's on 10 percent," Jewel said after finishing two back-to-back exams. Her mental battery for focus, motivation, and emotions was draining fast.

If you've ever had your phone die right when the group chat drama peaks—or just before you drop the perfect reaction GIF—you know that jolt of panic. You reach for a charger like your survival depends on it. ADHD energy works the same way. You have to notice when you're running low, be aware of what's draining you, and recharge before you crash.

"Some days it's like starting with a phone that barely holds a charge," Jewel explained. "I can go from 100 percent to low power mode before lunch. Stuff that looks small to other people—answering a text, leaving the house on time, even picking out clothes—can eat up way more of my charge than I realize."

It's not just about keeping your charge; it's about knowing *where* it's going. That's where the Solve-It Grid comes in. It's like a map for your brain's battery life. It showed Jewel why a quick task, like checking her email, could drain her fast–while something else, like putting on a playlist and re-arranging her room, energized her.

For Jewel, the grid made the pattern clear: *This task drains me. That one refuels me.* And it's not just Jewel. People with ADHD everywhere can use this same map to spot their own patterns. Every task lands somewhere on the grid, based on two things: how fun it feels and how much emotional fuel it carries.

The grid is split into four quadrants. Each one shows how your brain spends or gains energy. Some zones drain your battery fast, some help you recharge, and some just leave you stuck in the annoying in-between. We'll start with Yellow and Red because those are the zones where ADHD energy gets tangled the most–tasks either drain you fast or feel impossible to begin.

The Solve-It Grid

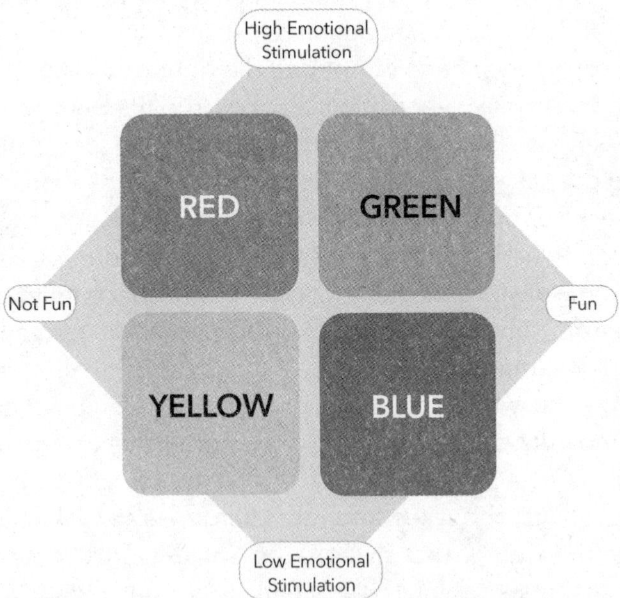

The Yellow Quadrant

On the Solve-It Grid, the Yellow Quadrant is where you place tasks that are not fun and have low emotional intensity. Tasks in this quadrant just sit there like a soggy piece of toast.

You've met Yellow before:

- folding laundry that's been sitting in a basket for three days
- logging into a homework portal to type a single sentence of a discussion post
- clearing out your cloud storage because you keep getting warnings

Yellow tasks don't usually drain your battery fast, but they *feel* like they will, which is why they're so easy to avoid. Just thinking about them can make you want to open Instagram,

Yellow Zone Friction

- What in your life feels like a Yellow task right now?
- What are you avoiding, even though you know it matters?
- What's one way to make that task smaller, faster, or easier so it's not such a drain?

reorganize your apps, or wander into the kitchen to see if there's leftover pizza.

That's where Lenora, a high school senior I worked with, was stuck. She hated Yellow tasks because they felt like a waste of time. But when she broke down her AP Lit reading–fifteen pages at a time with a twenty-minute timer–she was surprised to find it wasn't that bad. She didn't finish everything, but she made real progress and still had energy left.

The danger with Yellow is that if you ignore it long enough, it mutates into Red. This is the panic zone, where your brain finally jumps in, but at a brutal cost to your energy.

The Red Quadrant

The Red Quadrant is where you put tasks that aren't fun and come loaded with emotional intensity. These are the jobs you don't enjoy, and your brain reacts to them with a surge of energy–usually from stress, worry, or frustration. That jolt can push you into action, but it's like sprinting on low power mode: You burn through the charge fast.

You've probably been here before:

- forgetting to turn in an online assignment until the portal's about to close
- realizing your uniform's still in the laundry right before the game
- checking the project rubric the night before it's due and discovering you're missing half the requirements

In the moment, Red can feel powerful. You get the rush of *Oh no, I have to do this now*, and it propels you forward. But that energy is expensive, and the crash afterward hits hard.

You might get hooked on Red because it tricks you into feeling productive. You wait, pressure builds, you sprint to the finish, and—boom—you get that "I did it!" high. Over time, your brain starts to crave the chaos as the only way to get moving.

Malik swears he works better under pressure. He'll ignore an assignment for days, then grind it out at 3:00 a.m. The adrenaline rush gets him through, but it trains his brain to depend on stress instead of steady focus.

The Red Quadrant isn't "bad." Sometimes intense emotions give you the push you need. But if Red is your main way of powering through, you're training your brain to run on stress—and stress isn't a sustainable fuel source. When that stress finally burns you out, your brain goes looking for relief. That's where Blue comes in—the easy, low-pressure zone that feels like recovery.

Red Zone Reality Check

- What tasks do you *always* push aside until the panic hits?
- What emotion usually kicks you into gear—worry, frustration, anger?
- Can you start earlier with a smaller spark instead of waiting for Red?

The Blue Quadrant

The Blue Quadrant is where you put tasks that are fun and low in emotional intensity. They're easy, low-effort activities you enjoy. Blue can be great for recovery.

Blue activities are like putting your brain on a slow charger. They're relaxing ways to refill:

- watching a couple of episodes of a comfort show
- playing a casual game on your phone
- lying in a hammock listening to music

A little Blue is refreshing. It's like fries when you're only a little hungry: A small serving hits the spot, but too much leaves you stuffed and sleepy.

Liam loved his Blue time because it felt safe. "I need this," he told me. And he was right—we all need space to chill.

Blue Zone Balance

- What Blue activities recharge you?

- Which ones leave you drained?

- How can you set a boundary (an episode count, a timer) so Blue stays a break and doesn't turn into a stall?

After school, though, he'd hop online with friends "just for a little while." Hours later his homework was untouched. What started as a recharge had quietly slid into avoidance.

Blue works best when it has boundaries. Two episodes, a fifteen-minute scroll, a quick game—enough to reset your brain, not derail your day. Drag it out too long, and your rest time stops restoring you. Instead of recharging, you're stuck in slow motion.

Blue is useful, but it's a slow charge. If you want your battery to power back up faster and leave you energized, you need Green.

The Green Quadrant

Green is your happy place—the quadrant where tasks are both fun and full of emotional lift. These are the things that make you feel alive, connected, or inspired.

Green looks different for everyone, but it often involves creativity, connection, or meaning, like:

- spending an afternoon with friends you can be completely yourself around
- working on a project you care about
- playing your sport on a perfect-weather day

The power of Green is how quickly it restores you. It's like plugging your brain into a fast charger—you walk away lighter, grounded, and more yourself. Green moments leave you with memories worth keeping and not another blur of scrolling. In Green, you come out with more energy than you started with—and often a brighter mood too.

The tricky part is that Green usually takes a little effort up front. Hanging out with friends, starting a project, or heading outside to play your sport can feel harder than just grabbing

Green Zone Refills

- What activities fill your battery fastest?

- How can you set them up ahead of time so they're easier to choose than Blue?

your phone. When you're running low, it's tempting to slide into Blue.

That's where Sam found himself. Mountain biking with friends always lifted his mood, but on many afternoons the couch and his phone won out instead. "I know biking would help," he admitted, "but scrolling takes zero effort." More time in Blue, less in Green, and his battery never made it back to full strength.

Blue helps you coast. Green helps you soar. If you want a true recharge, Green is where it happens.

Thinking Through Your Tasks

Now that you know what each quadrant looks like, you can start using the grid to make smarter energy moves.

Say you've realized the thing you need to do is sitting squarely in Yellow. Oof. Not exactly your dream starting point. Before you groan and shove it to the bottom of your list, pause and ask why you don't want to touch it. Sometimes the reason is simple: It's boring. Other times there's more underneath. Finding the real reason makes it easier to figure out your next move. Here's a process you can use:

1. Spot the quadrant.
   Where does the task land—Yellow, Red, Blue, or Green?
2. Figure out what's stopping you.
   Mood hurdle: *Ugh, I hate this.*
   Missing gear: *I don't have what I need.*
   Missing info: *I don't even know how to start.*
3. Choose an action.

   If it's a mood hurdle:

   Add dopamine: Play your hype playlist, race a timer, or promise yourself a reward.

   Change the vibe: Move spots, grab a snack or drink, or reset your space.

   Pair it up: FaceTime a friend or body-double so it feels lighter.

   Reframe it: Remind yourself, *This is only ten minutes, then I'm done.*

   If it's missing gear:

   Grab the basics: Get your charger, book, or uniform—whatever's essential.

   Stage it: Lay things out where you'll need them (like clothes the night before).

   Make a kit: Keep a "ready kit" (pens, calculator, water bottle, gum, etc.) so it's one grab, not five trips.

   If it's missing info:

   Ask quick: Text a classmate, DM a friend, or ask a teacher.

Search smart: Google it, hit YouTube, or watch a quick tutorial.

Start with what you know: Do the part that makes sense, then loop back for help.

4. Write it down.

   ADHD brains burn energy trying to juggle instructions in working memory. Write down even the obvious steps. Putting steps in order clears the clutter and frees up focus for doing the task.

When you know where a task lands on the quadrant, you don't get blindsided by drains or detours. You can guide your energy toward what matters most and still have fuel left for the things that make you feel alive.

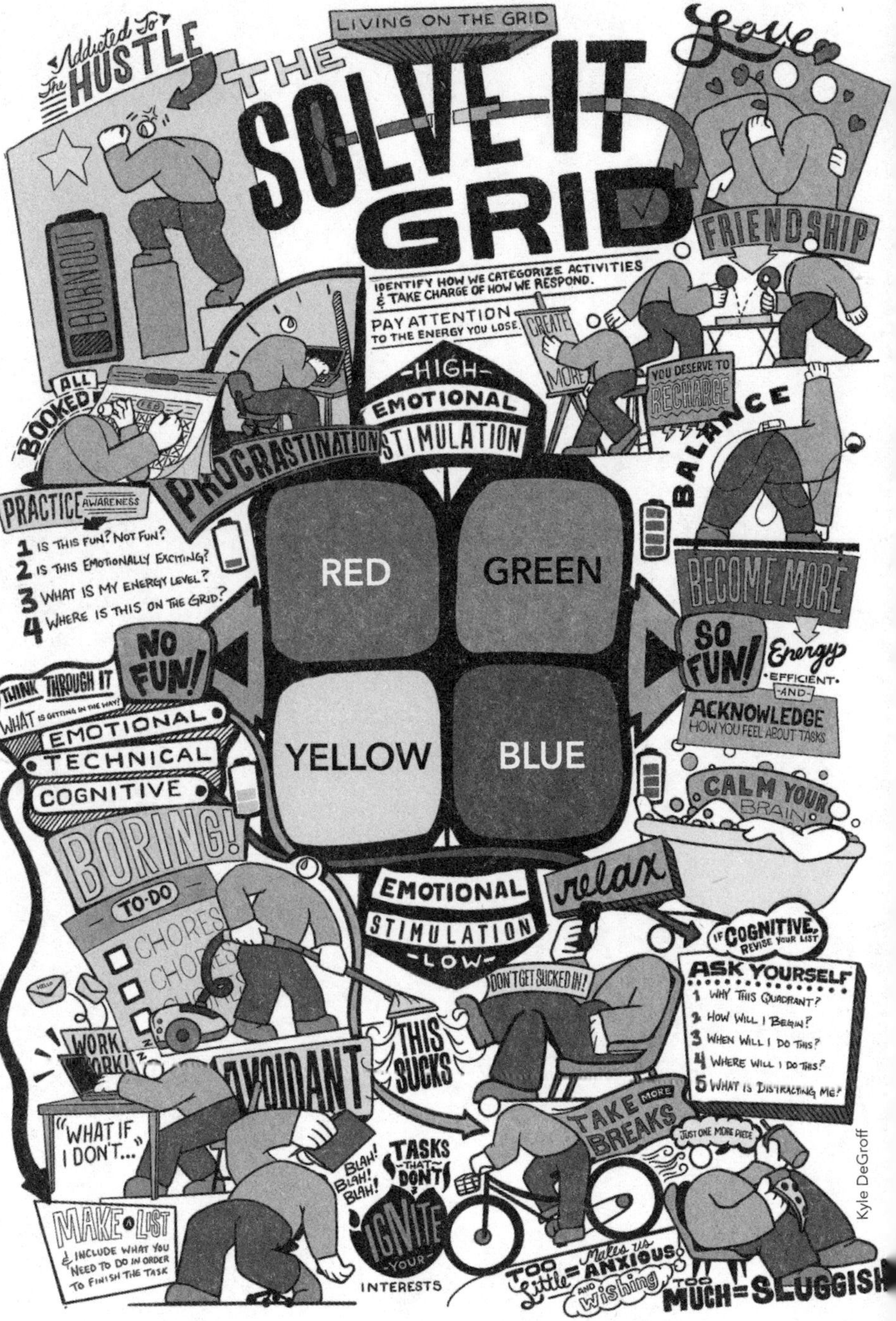

Kyle DeGroff

8

Patterns That Mess with Your Battery

Motivation with ADHD is full of habits you fall into without thinking. Once you see your habits, you can start untangling them and replace them with habits that actually work for you. Below are four common patterns I see with ADHD brains. As you read them, notice which ones sound most like you.

The Need-for-Speed Pattern

Malik insists he works better under pressure. It's not only with schoolwork–he waits until the last possible minute to fill out a college application, walks into soccer practice seconds before warm-ups, and flies into his restaurant shift right as he needs to punch in. "It's like my brain needs a countdown to kick in," he says.

Malik spends a lot of time in the Red Quadrant of the Solve-It Grid, where tasks aren't fun but still get your emotions buzzing. Red isn't restful; it's the high-alert zone. It feels urgent, important, or competitive enough to make your brain fire up fast.

Quick Self-Check: THE NEED-FOR-SPEED PATTERN

Give yourself 1 point for every yes answer.

__ 1. Do you always seem to have some kind of crisis going on (real or exaggerated)?
__ 2. Does getting angry or frustrated sometimes help you power through work?
__ 3. Do you often feel rushed and have a jam-packed schedule?
__ 4. Would friends or family say you get into big conflicts or have intense reactions?
__ 5. Do you feel guilty if you use free time to just relax?
__ 6. Do you need to win to enjoy games or sports?
__ 7. Do you usually walk, eat, or move quickly?
__ 8. Do you feel energized when a deadline is looming?
__ 9. Do you often double-book yourself or run late because you overcommit?
__ 10. Does calm or quiet ever feel boring or even uncomfortable to you?

Scoring:

0–3: You dabble in this pattern.
4–6: It shows up a lot.
7–10: You probably lean hard on this pattern, and it might be worth learning how to slow down.

This is the Need-for-Speed pattern. You wait until the stakes are high, the timer is running out, or the challenge feels intense before you engage. High emotional intensity gives your brain chemistry a boost from dopamine and adrenaline that makes focus easier. Without that boost, tasks can feel flat and hard to start.

For many with ADHD, this strategy "works" . . . until it doesn't. Living in Red can be thrilling, but it's also exhausting. You're constantly reacting instead of pacing yourself, always running on crisis fuel. And if you work only when the clock is ticking down, your brain starts to believe it needs that rush to function at all.

The Need-for-Speed pattern shows up in both big and small ways. You might pack your schedule so tight that you're always rushing, wait until the very last moment to start an assignment, or lean on competition and deadlines just to feel the rush. Sometimes this even looks like picking fights or stirring up drama—without meaning to—because the conflict gives your brain a jolt of energy. At first, the Need-for-Speed pattern feels exciting. But over time, it drains your battery, wears down your body, and puts extra strain on your relationships.

If this feels familiar, you might think, *Okay, I'll just stop doing everything last-minute*. But if your brain has learned to work only under high pressure, you can't flip that switch overnight. You have to retrain your brain to start without the rush.

1. *Spot the belief.* The Need-for-Speed pattern is often fueled by a hidden thought like, *I can only get things done in panic mode*. Notice when you are tempted to overcommit, and ask yourself, *Is this important—or just making me feel busy?*

2. *Try a reset.* Before you dive into the Red zone, take ten minutes to calm your body and brain. Breathe slowly, doodle, journal, or stretch.
3. *Check in with your body.* Running in Red makes you forget you even have a body. Ask yourself, *Do I need food, water, or a break? Are my shoulders tense? Is my jaw tight?*
4. *Start smaller.* Break projects into mini deadlines. Use a twenty-minute timer for a controlled countdown. Practice starting at 70 percent readiness instead of waiting for panic mode.
5. *Balance your fuel.* Pair Red activities with Green ones that recharge you. After the sprint of a Red activity, give yourself time in a space that restores your energy quickly, not a Blue zone slow charge.

Not everyone intentionally seeks pressure like this. Some follow a different rhythm of waiting long enough for boring tasks to become emergencies, known as the Playing-with-Fire pattern.

The Playing-with-Fire Pattern

The Playing-with-Fire pattern occurs when you have a dull Yellow Quadrant task, and instead of starting, you delay until it escalates into a full-blown Red emergency. At first, it seems harmless—just a minor delay. But then the deadline approaches, pressure increases, and suddenly you're battling a fire you could have extinguished days ago.

Gia, a first-year college student, fell into this trap constantly. She'd look at a small, low-interest assignment and think, *I'll start later*. Days would pass. The task would creep from Yellow to orange to full-blown Red. "I don't know why

I do this," she said. "I finally get it done, but I feel awful afterward—like I let myself down."

The Playing-with-Fire pattern doesn't give you the thrill of the Need-for-Speed pattern. Instead, it leaves you drained,

Quick Self-Check: THE PLAYING-WITH-FIRE PATTERN

Give yourself 1 point for every yes answer.

__ 1. Do you often rush to finish tasks you meant to start earlier?

__ 2. Do you delay simple tasks that would take only a few minutes?

__ 3. Do you waste time on other things when you should be prepping for a deadline?

__ 4. Are you constantly saying, "I'll do it tomorrow"?

__ 5. Do you get lost in little, low-priority details before tackling the real thing?

__ 6. Even after deciding what to do, do you put off starting?

__ 7. Do you often run out of time completely?

__ 8. Does fear of making mistakes keep you from getting started?

__ 9. Do you make excuses for not doing your best work?

__ 10. After avoiding a task, do you punish yourself by cutting out fun (like hanging out or gaming)?

Scoring:

0–3: You flirt with this pattern.

4–6: It's a recurring issue.

7–10: This pattern might be running the show—and burning more of your energy than you realize.

guilty, and frustrated. And sometimes you punish yourself by skipping the fun and restorative activities of Green because you feel like you don't deserve them.

If this is your pattern, you already know how it goes. You delay the boring Yellow task, it turns into Red, you panic and scramble, and afterward you're wiped out and frustrated. Here's how to break the cycle:

1. *Spot the belief.* The sneaky thought is usually, *I work best under pressure.* It feels true because the panic finally makes you move. But that's not "best"; that's borrowing tomorrow's energy. Notice when your brain says, *I'll start later* or *I need the deadline to focus*, and call it out before it lights the match.
2. *Shrink the task.* Yellow tasks often look giant and shapeless, which makes your brain dodge them. Slice them into pieces so small they feel almost silly. Instead of "Write my essay," try "Open a new doc and type the title." Once you're moving, the fire loses its fuel.
3. *Try the ten-minute rule.* Tell yourself you only have to work on the Yellow task for ten minutes. Set a timer. Worst case, you chipped away at it. Best case, you find your flow and keep going. Either way, you beat the panic spiral.
4. *Do a reality check.* Look at your list and ask, *Which Yellow items are already sliding toward Red?* Be honest—are you avoiding the task or the feelings around it? That quick reality check can stop a flicker from turning into flames.
5. *Reward yourself with Green.* Don't punish yourself by cutting out fun. Instead, use Green Quadrant activities—like hopping on Discord, watching an

episode, or shooting hoops—as fuel. A little reward keeps you moving without burning you out.

6. *Borrow accountability.* Still stuck? Pull someone else in. Text a friend: *Starting my math homework at 3:00—ask me if I did it.* Sometimes a simple check-in is enough to keep the spark from catching.

The Playing-with-Fire pattern uses avoidance as a survival strategy. The more you practice tackling Yellow before it turns Red, the more you'll prove to yourself that you don't need panic mode to get things done.

The Red, Blue, and Back Again Pattern

The Red, Blue, and Back Again pattern feels like emotional whiplash. You push yourself into Red—hyperfocused, stressed, and running hot—until you burn out completely. Then you crash into Blue, zoning out with Netflix, scrolling, or sleep. And when you start to recover, guilt or panic slingshots you back into Red, and the cycle repeats.

Elena, a high school junior, lived this pattern all semester. She'd spend days in Red mode—cranking out projects, staying late at rehearsal, working her part-time job—until she literally fell asleep at the dinner table. Then she'd sink into Blue for an entire weekend, gaming and scrolling until her eyes hurt. By Monday morning, panic yanked her back into Red again. "It's like I'm either sprinting or face-planting," she said. "There's no middle ground."

At first, this back-and-forth can look like balance—you're working hard in Red and "resting" in Blue. But the extremes leave you drained, disconnected, and always behind.

If this sounds like you, it might feel like you have only two speeds: all-out or checked out. Elena realized this after crashing midsemester. Instead of pushing herself into

Quick Self-Check: THE RED, BLUE, AND BACK AGAIN PATTERN

Give yourself 1 point for every yes answer.

__ 1. Do you swing from working nonstop to totally shutting down?

__ 2. Do you push toward goals but rarely feel joy in reaching them?

__ 3. Do you know you should be working but feel too drained to start?

__ 4. Do you flip between overreacting one day and not caring the next?

__ 5. Do you often feel an urgency that won't let you relax?

__ 6. Do people say you have only two speeds—on and off?

__ 7. Do you forget to enjoy the process because you're focused on the push?

__ 8. Do you regret missing the "good parts" because of overwork or burnout?

__ 9. Do you rest only when your body forces you to—like when you get sick?

__ 10. Do you sometimes use Blue zone activities (like scrolling or gaming) as a way to hide how exhausted you are?

Scoring:

0–3: You probably balance your energy pretty well.

4–6: You may be swinging between extremes more than you realize.

7–10: This pattern is likely running the show—and draining more of your battery than you think.

another Red streak, she started adding one Green activity between big pushes, like grabbing tacos with friends before rehearsal. That tiny reset stopped her from hitting Blue and gave her enough energy to enjoy what she was doing.

Here are a few ways to break the cycle:

1. *Spot the belief.* Notice when your brain says, *I can't stop now.* Remind yourself that slowing down protects your energy.
2. *Mix your colors.* Don't live in Red until you collapse into Blue. Add a small Yellow task (like putting away laundry) or a Green one (like shooting hoops) to steady yourself.
3. *Set a stop time.* Pick a cutoff in the evening, even if your list isn't done. Protecting tomorrow's energy is more powerful than squeezing out one more Red sprint.
4. *Check in.* Ask yourself, *Am I all Red right now?* If the answer is yes, throw in ten minutes of Green or Yellow. Even a tiny shift keeps the swing from getting extreme.
5. *Reconnect.* Rapid swings between Red and Blue can be hard on friends and family. One day your emotions are intense and consuming, and the next you're pulling away. Build in steady Green time with people you trust so relationships don't get lost in the chaos.

Breaking this pattern isn't about becoming less ambitious or less chill. It's about balance. The more you practice adding small doses of Yellow and Green, the less you'll find yourself trapped between burnout and shutdown—and the more energy you'll have left for the good stuff.

For some with ADHD, Red feels like too much and they avoid it. Instead of bouncing between the two extremes, they retreat into their comfort zone and stay there. That's the Nothin'-but-Blue pattern.

The Nothin'-but-Blue Pattern

Some ADHD brains escape into the Blue Quadrant and camp out there. Blue isn't bad; it's the chill zone: scrolling, gaming, hanging out, resting. Everyone needs a little Blue time. But when you live there full-time, your battery doesn't recharge. It's like plugging your phone into a sketchy cord—you gain a little charge, but not enough to power the stuff that matters.

T.J. could run entire squads in *Call of Duty: Warzone* and knew every loadout in *Modern Warfare*. But in real life? Homework was ignored. Chores were dodged. Talking to a teacher about a late assignment? No way.

When I asked him about it, he shrugged. "It's easier to just . . . not," he said.

Blue felt safe to T.J.—no pressure, no judgment, no uncomfortable feelings. But the cost was real. His grades slipped, his parents stopped trusting him, and deep down he felt stuck.

That's the Nothin'-but-Blue pattern: avoiding Red or Yellow so much that you numb out in low-effort distractions. If procrastination is like waiting until the last second before sprinting, then Blue is when you don't even lace up your shoes. At first, it feels cozy. Stay too long, though, and you end up restless, disconnected, and disappointed in yourself.

If you spend a lot of time in Blue, it's not because you're lazy. This quadrant often feels safer than dealing with stress or the risk of failure. The goal isn't to ditch Blue but to step out of it enough to keep growing.

Quick Self-Check: THE NOTHIN'-BUT-BLUE PATTERN

Give yourself 1 point for every yes answer.

__ 1. Do you question why schoolwork or chores "have to be so hard" and then skip them?

__ 2. Do you wait for "inspiration" but kill time with YouTube, Snapchat, or games?

__ 3. Do you default to fun when you know responsibilities are waiting?

__ 4. Do you avoid tasks unless you're sure you'll nail them?

__ 5. Do you imagine people criticizing your work before you've even started?

__ 6. Do you avoid social situations because you're afraid of messing up?

__ 7. Do you turn down opportunities because they feel risky or embarrassing?

__ 8. Do you stay in Blue so long that you feel stuck or guilty afterward?

__ 9. Do you tell yourself, "I'll deal with it later," but never circle back?

__ 10. Do you use Blue time as a way to avoid uncomfortable feelings like stress, shame, or boredom?

Scoring:

0–3: You probably use Blue in a balanced way.
4–6: Blue might be your go-to escape.
7–10: You may be living in Blue full-time—and it's keeping you from what you care about.

1. *Spot the belief.* Blue often comes with hidden thoughts like, *If I can't do it perfectly, I won't do it at all* and *If I stay in Blue, I can't fail.* Notice when your brain feeds you those lies.
2. *Name your Blue.* What's your default escape? Instagram? Gaming? Doodling? Try going one day without it—or set a timer for it—to see how hooked you are.
3. *Play the Yellow–Blue game.* Work on a Yellow task for twenty minutes, then give yourself ten minutes of Blue. Timers help. Many people find once they start Yellow, they don't want to stop.
4. *Stack tiny wins.* Pick three easy Yellow steps each day (like "put my backpack by the door" or "write the essay title"). Small progress builds momentum.
5. *Trade one Blue for Green.* Swap one Blue activity for something energizing—going for a walk, FaceTiming, or shooting baskets. Green fills your battery; Blue just passes time.

The Nothin'-but-Blue pattern doesn't mean something's wrong with you; it means you've learned to hide from the

Need-for-Speed: Living in Red can feel thrilling, but it drains your battery faster than it refills.

Playing-with-Fire: Putting off Yellow until it turns Red only fuels panic, not progress.

Red, Blue, and Back Again: Running full throttle and then crashing isn't balance; it's burnout on repeat.

Nothin'-but-Blue: Blue feels safe, but too much keeps you stuck instead of recharged.

hard stuff. The more you practice dipping into Yellow and Green, the less stuck you'll feel—and the more your battery will recharge.

These patterns are energy shortcuts your brain has learned. Shortcuts can be swapped for better and more effective habits.

These patterns also don't define who you are. They're habits your brain has built to manage motivation and energy in the moment. Sometimes they look like chasing the rush, waiting for panic, burning out, or hiding in comfort. But these patterns aren't permanent settings. The moment you can see one, you've already started to change it.

The next step is learning how to steer your energy more intentionally. That's where the Solve-It Grid comes in. It gives you a clear map of how tasks land in your brain—what drains you, what restores you, and what helps you move forward.

PREDICTABLE PATTERNS
IDENTIFY PATTERNS
THE SOLVE IT GRID
WE CAN GET STUCK IN THESE BEHAVIOR PATTERNS THAT KEEP US FROM USING OUR RESOURCES WELL.
-HIGH- EMOTIONAL STIMULATION
NEED FOR SPEED
PANIC
THE "NEED FOR SPEED" PATTERN CREATES TENSION & PRESSURE.
IT'S VERY STRESSFUL FOR YOUR BODY!
NO FUN!
SO FUN!
MANUFACTURED
CRISIS
CAN'T STOP WON'T STOP
WORK BEST UNDER PRESSURE
BACK TO WORK!
EMOTIONAL STIMULATION -LOW-
NOTHIN' BUT BLUE
DIFFERENT THAN PROCRASTINATION
AVOIDS YELLOW & RED TASKS
YOU CAN DO BETTER
LATE!
RED, BLUE AND BACK AGAIN
ALL OR NOTHING
EMOTIONAL ROLLERCOASTER
MAYBE I'LL JUST PLAY VIDEO GAMES INSTEAD...
WORK
playing WITH FIRE!
TIME'S UP!
TO-DO
THE ENDLESS Loop = FRANTIC IN RED
TIRED? GO BLUE...
GET BACK TO RED!
CRASHED
100%
0%
THIS YELLOW TASK IS BORING. I'LL WAIT UNTIL IT BECOMES RED
NEVER-ENDING
WHICH PATH will YOU CHOOSE

9

From Crash Zone to In the Zone

Ali's phone buzzed with a text: *Meet me outside—don't forget the HDMI cord.*

Cord? What cord? Her stomach dropped. *Wait . . . our presentation? Today?* In a heartbeat her pulse was thudding, her thoughts colliding, all ending in the same awful conclusion: *I blew it.*

That's how quickly an ADHD mind can swing from calm to chaos. One moment you're steady, the next your heart is pounding and your emotions shove logic out of the way.

It feels random, like your brain has turned against you. But there's a pattern. That's what the ADHD Emotional Health Ladder shows: how stress, emotions, and ADHD stack together step-by-step, and how each level shifts the way you think and act.

The Emotional Health Ladder

Level 1: Calm and clear
Level 2: Steady and engaged
Level 3: Doing, not steering
Level 4: Urgent and scattered
Level 5: Frozen or explosive

The ADHD Emotional Health Ladder

The ladder has five levels: two clearheaded levels at the top, one middle level, and two reactive levels at the bottom. At the top, you're steady and calm, with the most access to your thinking brain. As you move down, stress and emotion start calling more of the shots, and your behavior shifts along with them. Knowing where you are on the ladder gives you a chance to pause, steady yourself, and climb back up.

Here are the five levels:

Level 1: In the Zone (Clearheaded). You're calm, steady, and fully present. You can choose how to respond instead of reacting.

Level 2: Locked In (Mostly Clearheaded). You're engaged and focused without being flooded. Emotions give you signals, but they're not in charge.

Level 3: Autopilot (Middle Zone). You're getting things done but not really present. You're reactive and going through the motions, missing signals from your body or other people.

Level 4: Panic Mode (Reactive). Fight, flight, freeze, or fawn kicks in. Your pulse is racing, your thoughts are scattering, and your eyes are locked on the problem like it's life-and-death, even when it isn't.

Level 5: Crash Zone (Highly Reactive). Your brain feels like it's short-circuiting, and you might lash out or shut down completely. Either way, you end up saying or doing things that you don't mean and wish you could take back.

Before reading the text message, Ali bounced between Level 2, *Locked In*, and Level 3, *Autopilot*. Sometimes she was focused, highlighting notes in class and feeling in control. Other times she would rush through tasks, moving quickly without realizing how stressed she was becoming.

After the reminder text, she dropped into Level 4, *Panic Mode*. Her pulse spiked, her thoughts scattered, and she quickly spiraled further into Level 5, *Crash Zone*—where emotions take over and she reacts in ways that don't feel like herself.

That's how the Emotional Health Ladder works. You don't always notice yourself moving down one step at a time; it feels like you're fine one minute and falling apart the next. But the ladder provides a way to pause, recognize where you are, and steady yourself.

Naming your level offers choices. At the top, you have the clearest access to your calm brain and your best decisions. As you move down, emotions become louder and your thinking brain quiets. But even one small action—taking a few breaths, texting a friend, or breaking a task into smaller parts—can help you shift upward. Every step you climb brings more calm, more clarity, and more control.

Now that you've seen the entire ladder, let's zoom in. The middle zone—Level 3, Autopilot—is the tipping point. From here, you can either return to calm or drift further into overload.

The Emotional Health Ladder

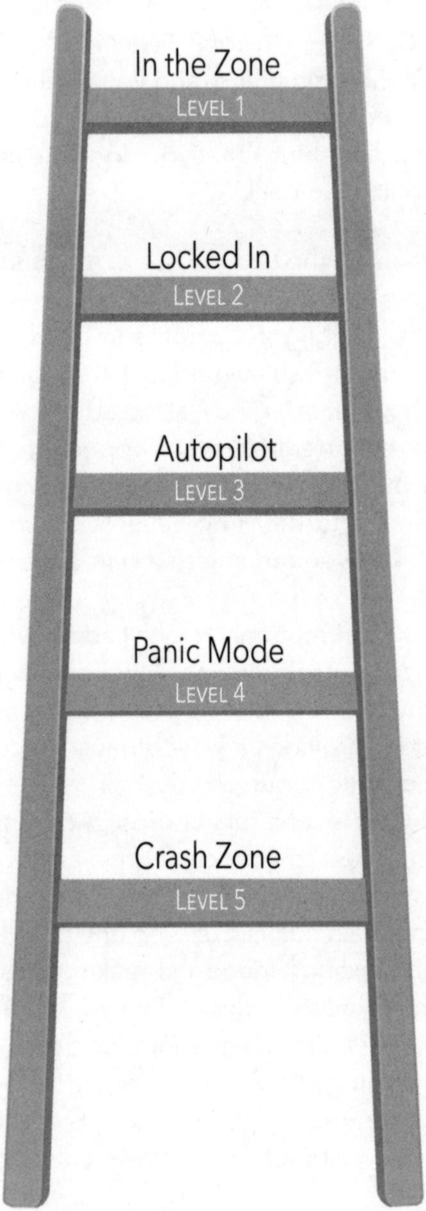

Level 3: Autopilot (Middle Zone)

Most of us spend large parts of the day at this level. It's called *Autopilot* because you're not really choosing your thoughts or actions; you're reacting to whatever comes up. A notification buzzes; you check it. The teacher assigns homework; you jot it down. A friend texts; you reply. You're moving, but you're not steering.

From the outside, Autopilot seems fine. You're busy checking off boxes and maybe even appearing productive. But beneath the surface, your day is running you instead of the other way around.

Your brain gets so focused on doing that it forgets to stop and ask, *Am I okay? Do I need a break? Am I even working on the right thing?*

ADHD minds at Level 3 become obsessed with efficiency. I can hear some of you saying, "Wait, isn't that a good thing?" Sure–except efficiency without awareness comes with a cost. You overlook hunger cues, ignore how tired you are, or suppress feelings that warn you're overloaded. Stopping feels like falling behind, so you keep pushing forward. But Autopilot doesn't allow you to adjust. You check off tasks without noticing how you're doing–and that's when you can slip down the ladder.

Ali's week had been hectic, so without realizing it, she'd slipped into Autopilot. Every day blurred together with classes, assignments, and "yeah, I can do that" commitments. Her phone kept buzzing, her planner was overflowing, and she kept telling herself, "If I can just make it to the weekend, I'll be fine." But she wasn't. Her body was exhausted, her ADHD symptoms grew louder, and even hanging out with friends felt like another chore instead of a genuine break.

That's the hidden trap of Autopilot: You start treating people like items on a checklist instead of connections. It becomes "just do your part so I can do mine," rather than actually being present. You're physically there but mentally somewhere else—already halfway to the next task. And the second that life throws you a curveball—an unexpected text, a sudden change, someone needing your attention—Autopilot doesn't bend. It snaps. Emotions flood in, the system crashes, and you drop straight into Panic Mode.

Autopilot Moments

- **When was the last time you realized you were just going through the motions?**

- **What were you responding to most—notifications, expectations, other people?**

- **What signs did your body give that you were tired, hungry, tense, or overloaded?**

- **At what point did Autopilot stop helping and start costing you?**

Quick Check: AM I ON AUTOPILOT (MIDDLE ZONE)?

- ☐ I've gone through a whole day without really noticing how I felt.
- ☐ I pushed through hunger, tiredness, or stress instead of taking a break.
- ☐ I treated people like tasks to get done instead of actually connecting.
- ☐ I felt productive but also kind of empty or disconnected.
- ☐ A small change (like a text or schedule shift) threw me off more than it should have.

If you checked two or more boxes, you may be on Autopilot. Catching it matters—it's the first step to shifting into a level where you're steering.

Level 4: Panic Mode (Reactive)

Panic Mode is like the sudden drop on a roller coaster. Your stomach lurches, your body reacts before your mind catches up, and all you can think is *Hang on!* Your system senses danger—even if it's only a late assignment or a buzzing group text—and it slams into overdrive.

In this state, everything feels urgent. Your thoughts scatter, your emotions spike, and your attention system shifts into instinct mode. You're not calmly choosing what to do; you're reacting. That's why, for someone with ADHD, the swing often feels like whiplash—one moment steady, the next in chaos.

Jordan glanced at the clock—10:03 p.m.—and his stomach dropped. The paper he'd avoided all week was due tomorrow. Panic set in. *How did I forget? What if I fail? What if my teacher thinks I don't care?* His shoulders stiffened, his hands trembled, and he yanked out his laptop, typing furiously. By 2:00 a.m., the report was finished—but so was Jordan. He dragged himself to class exhausted, snapping at friends, convinced he'd already blown it.

From the outside, Panic Mode might seem productive. You might crank out an essay in a single night or clean the kitchen thoroughly before your parents arrive home. But that burst of energy comes from stress chemicals, not consistent focus—and the crash is hard. You end up exhausted, irritable, and more prone to errors.

Stress isn't steady fuel; it's more like a sugar rush. It spikes quickly and then drops you, leaving you drained and shaky. The more you rely on stress, the faster you fall into the Crash Zone.

Panic Mode Moments

- When was the last time your brain went into Panic Mode?
- What triggered it—a deadline, a text, a fight, something else?
- How did your body feel while it was happening?

Quick Check: AM I IN PANIC MODE (REACTIVE)?

- ☐ My thoughts are racing and I feel on edge.
- ☐ Everything feels like an emergency.
- ☐ I'm snappy or impatient with people.
- ☐ I'm working in a frantic burst and making mistakes.
- ☐ I'm exhausted but too wired to calm down.

If you checked two or more boxes, you may be in Panic Mode. This is a signal to take one step up the ladder. See the next chapter for how to move.

Level 5: Crash Zone (Highly Reactive)

Crash Zone is the lowest level of the Emotional Health Ladder, where your brain feels overwhelmed and out of control. Instead of your brain making steady decisions, your body takes over. You might freeze and shut down or snap and lash out.

Sometimes this manifests as paralysis—you can't think clearly, you can't get started, and even the smallest task feels impossible. Other times it appears as explosive reactions—snapping, overreacting, or pushing people away. Both are overwhelming and leave you drained afterward.

Your system is defending itself after being pushed too far. The relief is fleeting, though. Shutting down or exploding might seem like escape in the moment, but responsibilities build up, relationships strain, and shame sneaks in, making the climb back up more difficult.

Eli knew that feeling all too well. After a week of late nights and nonstop stress, he sat down to start his English project—and just froze. The cursor blinked on the empty screen like it was mocking him. He tried everything—five more minutes, one more video, one more snack—but his brain wouldn't budge. This wasn't procrastination; it was paralysis. His system was overloaded, and starting felt impossible. He drifted between panic and numbness until the night slipped away. By morning, the project was still untouched, and Eli wasn't only behind; he was buried in guilt.

For Jada, overload looked completely different. After she'd had a tough week of practices, assignments, and hardly any sleep, her younger brother casually asked if she could move her stuff off the kitchen table. A small, innocent request—yet Jada exploded. Her voice rose, and words spilled out sharp and fast, blaming him for everything that felt heavy in her life. Before she could stop herself, she had slammed her door, her heart pounding, tears streaming down her face. Deep inside, she knew it wasn't about the table. But at this level, even the smallest spark doesn't seem small at all. It feels like a fire.

Stuck in Crash Zone

Think back to a time when everything felt like too much.

- **What did you do to escape—scream, slam doors, scroll, sleep, zone out?**

- **How did you feel afterward—better, worse, or just numb?**

Quick Check:
AM I IN CRASH ZONE (HIGHLY REACTIVE)?

- ☐ My brain feels like it's short-circuiting–either racing too fast or going totally blank.
- ☐ Even tiny tasks feel impossibly heavy, like lifting a thousand pounds.
- ☐ I'm zoning out, scrolling, or pacing, but I can't make myself start.
- ☐ I snap or overreact to something small, then instantly regret what I said or did.
- ☐ I feel drained, guilty, or ashamed–like I'm not myself anymore.

If you checked two or more boxes, you may be in the Crash Zone. Begin with one small step forward. See the next chapter for how to move up the ladder.

Whether you freeze or explode, Crash Zone pushes you farthest from your steady, clearheaded self. It feels like relief in the moment, but it often leaves you with more to fix once the storm passes.

If Level 5 represents stress taking over your system, Level 2 illustrates the opposite–what it feels like to remain grounded and maintain your balance, even when life gets rough.

Level 2: Locked In (Mostly Clearheaded)

On the other side of overload is Level 2: Locked In–the steady zone where your brain has room to think and stay engaged. Here, you're truly present with what you're doing. The Butler is on the job, whiteboard in hand.

In Locked In, emotions still appear, but they act more like helpful signals than hijackers. Your brain might say, "This part could be tricky" or "Don't forget a snack." Instead of ignoring those signals or getting overwhelmed, you notice, adjust, and continue.

Your body also reveals this difference. Your breathing becomes more even, your shoulders relax, and your thoughts calm down. If something unexpected occurs–like a pop quiz or a sudden change in plans–you don't panic. You have enough margin to pause, regroup, and move forward.

Lena reached this zone during band practice. Usually, every missed note would send her into a loop–replaying it until her frustration drowned out the rest of the music. But this day felt different. When her reed squeaked, she noticed the tension creeping in, took a breath, circled the spot in her music to fix later, and kept going with the group. When her fingers stiffened and her lip ached, she would normally push until she snapped. This time, she rolled her shoulders back,

Finding Your Locked-In Zone

Think back to a time when you felt focused but not stressed.

- **What were you doing, and how did your body feel?**

- **What signals told you that you were steady and engaged, not just running on Autopilot?**

> **Quick Check:**
> **AM I LOCKED IN (MOSTLY CLEARHEADED)?**
>
> - ☐ I feel engaged, not overwhelmed.
> - ☐ Emotions are giving me signals, but they're not running the show.
> - ☐ My body feels steady—my breathing is easy and my muscles are relaxed.
> - ☐ I can switch tasks without freaking out.
> - ☐ I'm making progress and actually feel good about it.
>
> If you checked two or more boxes, you may be Locked In. This is where your brain does some of its best work.

stretched her hands during a pause, and stayed steady with the ensemble. By the end of rehearsal, she wasn't wrung out or defeated. She was present, balanced, and engaged.

Locked In is balance in motion—emotions guiding without overwhelming. It's not the crystal clarity of Level 1, but it's steady enough to let you choose where to put your energy instead of letting it scatter.

Level 1: In the Zone (Clearheaded)

At the top of the ladder is In the Zone—a state of calm alertness where everything just *clicks*. Unlike Locked In, where you *work* to steady your focus, this level feels effortless. Your attention lines up, your emotions cooperate, and you move without second-guessing.

Here, feelings don't control you; they guide you. Nervousness becomes fuel instead of fear. Excitement turns into momentum instead of chaos. You don't stop to analyze every sensation; you just keep going.

Being "In the Zone" doesn't mean life suddenly gets easy. It means you feel capable. Your body is relaxed but ready—your breathing is even, your mind clear, your reactions quick. You can dive into a task, shift directions fast, and adapt when something changes without losing your footing.

Mason felt this during a basketball game. Normally, one mistake would replay in his head—a missed shot haunting him, his frustration rising, his rhythm gone. But that day, something was different. From the first play, he was fully tuned in—reading the court, calling for passes, and moving with natural focus. When he bricked a three-pointer, he didn't spiral. He exhaled, reset, and was already sprinting back on defense. By the final buzzer, he wasn't just proud; he *felt like himself.*

In the Zone is your clearest state. You're not forcing focus or fighting spirals. You're present, grounded, and free to respond with confidence.

In the Zone Moments

- **Can you remember a time when everything seemed to click and flow?**
- **What helped you get there—a rhythm, the setting, or how you were feeling inside?**
- **How did your body let you know you were calm but ready?**

Quick Check: AM I IN THE ZONE (CLEARHEADED)?

- ☐ I feel calm, clear, and fully present.
- ☐ Emotions are flowing with me, not against me.
- ☐ My body feels relaxed but ready to move.
- ☐ I can adjust quickly when things change.
- ☐ I feel like I'm in sync with myself and the moment.

If you checked two or more boxes, you may be In the Zone. This is a great place to be. Notice what's working and stay with it.

Climbing with Confidence

From the top to the bottom of the ladder, your level affects how you think, feel, and act. The real skill isn't *staying* at Level 1; it's recognizing where you are and knowing how to climb.

The ADHD Emotional Health Ladder gives you a way to notice what's happening inside your mind and body in real time. Some days you move upward, some days you slip down, and sometimes you bounce between levels faster than you realize. That isn't failure; it's how an ADHD nervous system reacts. Now you have a way to see it.

You don't need to live at the very top. What matters is recognizing where you are and which direction you're heading. Once you can identify your rung, you can decide to pause and stabilize, move upward, or prevent yourself from sliding further. That awareness restores your control. Every time you see your rung and take one step upward, you prove to yourself that calm and clarity are achievable, even in the midst of ADHD chaos.

In the next chapter, you'll learn how to incorporate the Emotional Health Ladder into daily life—recognizing your patterns, catching yourself earlier, and practicing ways to climb back toward clarity when emotions try to drag you down.

10

How to Use the Emotional Health Ladder

Imagine entering a tough video game without knowing the map. You run in circles, fall into traps, and keep making the same mistakes until you finally figure it out. Now picture someone giving you the map that shows your position and your options. Suddenly you're not stuck; you're strategic.

The ADHD Emotional Health Ladder works the same way. It's a tool for recognizing your mental state and choosing your next step. With it, you can identify what's happening in the moment and respond intentionally.

But before you can climb, you need to understand your current position on the ladder. Your body and thoughts send signals that indicate exactly which level you're on.

Step 1: Spot the Signals

The first step is learning to notice yourself. You can't climb if you don't know where you're standing, and each level leaves

The Emotional Health Ladder

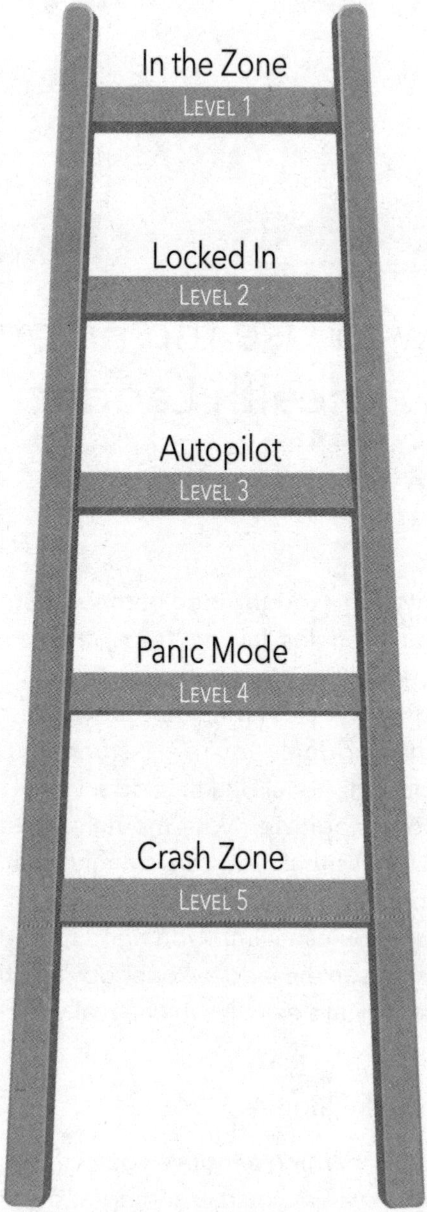

cues in your body, emotions, and self-talk. Sometimes those clues are subtle–tight shoulders, shallow breathing, or a quiet "don't mess this up" running in the background. Other times they're impossible to miss–losing hours to scrolling, snapping at a friend, or freezing in front of a simple assignment.

Your self-talk and emotions aren't random. They act as markers on the ladder. At the top, they feel like gentle nudges, such as "This might be tricky" or "Grab a snack before you crash." As you move lower, those nudges turn into shouts. Fear, anger, or exhaustion drown out your thinking brain until it's all alarm with no guidance.

Your body also shifts. Near the top, your breathing stays steady, your posture remains open, and ADHD traits feel manageable with strategies. As you move lower, tension starts to creep in–your shoulders tighten, your chest feels tight, your focus scatters, and your energy begins to drain. Symptoms become more intense as you rush, zone out, forget, or snap. At the very bottom, you either shut down completely or explode over something tiny. That shift isn't failure. It's feedback.

Think back to the stories from the last chapter.

Levels 1–3: Mason at Level 1 felt calm and steady, able to reset after a mistake. Lena at Level 2 noticed her shoulders tensing and circled a passage to keep from obsessing. Ali at Level 3 pushed through stress, restless and detached.

Levels 4–5: Jordan at Level 4 spiraled into panic, his body locking up even as he kept working. Eli and Jada at Level 5 hit the Crash Zone in different ways–Eli frozen in shame, Jada exploding in anger.

It might seem like a lot to monitor, but your body already has the sensors; you just need to practice noticing them. Start by asking yourself simple questions: *How does my body feel? What is my inner voice saying? What vibe is running through my self-talk right now?*

This is where the Signal Map comes into play. Check the sidebar for a quick cheat sheet of common cues at each level. Match what you're feeling to the list, and you can identify your level with confidence. The moment you do, you're already more in control.

Signal Map: Where Am I on the Ladder?

Level 1: In the Zone (Clearheaded)

- *Self-talk:* "Reset–next play." Clear, confident.
- *Emotions:* Calm, steady, in sync.
- *Body:* Breathing even, posture open, energy ready.
- *ADHD symptoms:* Still there, but manageable with strategies.

Level 2: Locked In (Mostly Clearheaded)

- *Self-talk:* "This might be tricky" or "Don't mess this up" flickering.
- *Emotions:* Small frustrations, but under control.
- *Body:* Mostly steady; shoulders start to rise, tension noticed and released.
- *ADHD symptoms:* An urge to redo mistakes, but strategies keep you engaged.

Level 3: Autopilot (Middle Zone)

- *Self-talk:* "Just get it done" or "I'll make it to the weekend."
- *Emotions:* Stress under the surface, low awareness.
- *Body:* Drained without realizing it–pushing through hunger, tiredness, or tension.
- *ADHD symptoms:* Busy but disconnected–forgetful, reactive, chasing urgency.

Level 4: Panic Mode (Reactive)

- *Self-talk:* "How did I forget?" or "What if I fail?" racing through.
- *Emotions:* Fear, urgency, defensiveness.
- *Body:* Jaw tight, heart pounding, hands shaky, body wired.
- *ADHD symptoms:* Frantic bursts of stress-fueled work, sloppy mistakes, exhaustion after.

Level 5: Crash Zone (Highly Reactive)

- *Self-talk:* "I can't . . ." or "This is too much."
- *Emotions:* Panic and shame (shutdown) or explosive anger (blowup).
- *Body:* Heavy and frozen (shutdown) or racing and shaky (blowup).
- *ADHD symptoms:* Total paralysis or outbursts; strategies gone, guilt and regret afterward.

Your Signals

- What signals usually show up first for you—self-talk, emotions, body cues, or ADHD symptoms?
- Can you recall a moment this week when those signals told you that you were slipping down the ladder?
- What level do you spend the most time on right now?

Step 2: Name Your Level

Once you've identified your signals, the next step is surprisingly powerful—specify your level on the ladder. Why does this matter? Because when you give your experience a name, you stop feeling lost inside it. Saying, "I'm in Level 3 right now" feels different from feeling scattered and stressed. It provides your brain with a handle to hold on to.

Naming your level isn't about judgment. Top isn't "good," and bottom isn't "bad." It's simply information about what's happening right now. Think of it like opening a map app. The blue dot isn't judging you; it's showing where you are so you can decide where to go next.

If you're torn between Level 3 and Level 4, pick the one that feels closest. The goal isn't precision but awareness. Once you can tag your level, you create enough space to choose your next move instead of being swept away by ADHD.

Use the Signal Map to check in with yourself. Read through the levels and see which one matches how you feel right now. Once you name it, you've already started shifting the game in your favor.

Naming your level gives you orientation. Step 3 is where awareness turns into action.

Step 3: Make One Move Up

Once you know your level, the next step is simple. What's one move that helps you climb a little higher? Just one shift upward.

The strength of the ladder is in its small resets—tiny actions that shift your brain and body from reactive to steadier ground. The goal isn't to reach instant calm but to move one rung higher. If you're stuck in Level 4 (Panic Mode), that

Quick Hack: How to Name Your Level

You don't need to analyze everything or get it "right." Just notice what fits best right now.

Start with one of these. You don't have to do all three.

1. Check your self-talk.

- Clear and encouraging–probably Level 1 or 2.
- Stressed or "just get it done"–likely Level 3.
- "What if I fail? I can't handle this"–sliding into Level 4.
- "I can't . . ." or "This is too much"–you're down at Level 5.

2. Notice your emotions.

- Balanced or steady–Level 1-2.
- Irritable or disconnected–Level 3.
- Fearful, urgent, or angry–Level 4.
- Panicked, shut down, exploding or blowing up–Level 5.

3. Check your body.

- Relaxed, with breathing steady–Level 1.
- A little tense, but catching it early–Level 2.
- Tired, restless, or pushing through–Level 3.
- Racing heart, tight stomach, locked muscles–Level 4.,
- Frozen (heavy) or jittery (shaky)–Level 5.

might mean saying, "Okay, just open the doc." If you're at Level 5 (Crash Zone), maybe all you can manage is a leg stretch or a sip of water.

Find one reset mode that truly works for you. You have four channels to test–body, emotion, self-talk, and ADHD resets.

Body Resets

Do box breathing–inhale for 4, hold for 4, exhale for 4, hold for 4 (or use a breathing app).

Shake it out–your arms, legs, and whole body, like you're clearing static.

Do a power reset–wall push-ups, squats, or planks.

Change the temp–step outside, grab an ice cube, or hold a hot mug.

Dance to your hype song from start to finish.

Emotion Resets

Do a 5-4-3-2-1 grounding trick (see, feel, hear, smell, taste).

Live-caption your brain–either record or write your thoughts. No editing, just spill.

Song swap–blast a hype track, then follow with a calmer one.

Take a laugh break–scroll one meme or watch a short clip.

Do a quick art plunge–sketch, doodle, or color for five minutes.

Self-Talk Resets

Flip "I can't" into "I can try one step."

Call it out–"That's stress talking, not me."

Write the thought down, then cross it out and replace it with a truer one.

Look at notes you've left for yourself–"I've done hard things before" or "Reset and move."

Record a pep talk to yourself and play it back.

ADHD Resets

Make it stupid-small–open the doc and write one word or set a two-minute timer.

Make a when/then deal–"When I finish this problem, then I get my phone."

Switch it up–try a new room, headphones, or a lighting shift.

Gamify it–race the timer, earn a point, or challenge a friend to a sprint.

Every small move upward gives you an opportunity to think more clearly. The higher you go, the easier the next move feels. The point isn't climbing perfectly; it's knowing you can always shift upward, no matter where you start.

Now let's put those four channels to work with more ideas for each level.

Level 5: Crash Zone

- *Self-talk:* Switch "I can't" to "I can try one small thing."
- *Emotions:* Say out loud, "This feels huge because I'm overloaded." Naming it takes the edge off.
- *Body:* Splash cold water on yourself, stretch, or hold an ice cube to jolt your system.
- *ADHD reset:* Pick the tiniest starter step–open the doc and type your name or set a two-minute timer.

Level 4: Panic Mode

- *Self-talk:* Remind yourself, *I only need to handle the next step, not the whole thing.*
- *Emotions:* Dump the worry onto paper–get it out of your head.

- *Body:* Try box breathing (inhale for 4, hold for 4, exhale for 4, hold for 4) or take a one-minute walk.
- *ADHD reset:* Break the task into one clear chunk and start there.

Level 3: Autopilot

- *Self-talk:* Replace "Just push through" with "Pause, then choose."
- *Emotions:* Ask yourself, *How am I feeling right now?*
- *Body:* Check the basics–do you need a snack, water, or a stretch?
- *ADHD reset:* Stop multitasking. Do one thing with intention, or try body-doubling with a friend.

Level 2: Locked In

- *Self-talk:* Encourage yourself–*Steady is good enough.*
- *Emotions:* Catch small frustrations–*This is tricky, but I can handle it.*
- *Body:* Roll your shoulders back, breathe deep, reset your posture.
- *ADHD reset:* Stick with your strategy–circle the tricky part, then keep going.

Level 1: In the Zone

- *Self-talk:* Remind yourself, *I'm clear and capable.*
- *Emotions:* Enjoy the calm confidence–it's fuel.
- *Body:* Keep noticing what feels steady–relaxed breath, ready energy.
- *ADHD reset:* Use this clarity for something meaningful, not just busywork.

Which Tools Work for You?

- **Which of these tools feels most natural to try when you're stressed?**
- **Which one do you already use without realizing it?**
- **What tool could you practice this week when you notice yourself sliding down the ladder?**

Practicing the Ladder

When you find yourself stressing about being late for the bus or zoning out during chores, see that as a chance to practice. Every small challenge you handle in daily life builds your ability to stay calm under pressure.

Maya thought about the ladder during algebra. Usually, one wrong answer would send her straight into Panic Mode. But this time, she recognized the signs—her shoulders tensed, and her brain was yelling, *You're dumb, you'll never get this.* She paused, took a breath, and told herself, *Okay, I'm at Level 4. Just try the next step.* Instead of spiraling, she climbed one rung. By the end of class, she hadn't solved everything perfectly, but she stayed steady enough to keep going. That small climb reminded her she didn't have to wait for panic to pass; she could practice moving upward right in the middle of it.

The more you practice, the more natural it becomes. Over time, the ladder stops being a diagram in your mind and becomes second nature—how you shift, reset, and move without overthinking. You'll recognize your signals faster, identify your level more quickly, and understand which small move helps you climb upward.

The ladder isn't about never slipping. It's about knowing you can recover, reset, and keep climbing.

CLIMBING THE LADDER
CULTIVATING
EMOTIONAL
HEALTH
HEALTHY TRAITS = TOP OF THE LADDER
USE THIS TO ASSESS WHERE YOU ARE & ADDRESS YOUR BEHAVIOR
IN THE ZONE
STATE OF PERPETUAL "PRESENCE." A QUIET MIND IN TOUCH WITH PRESENT MOMENT. RESPONDING TO TASKS, PEOPLE, SITUATIONS THE WAY WE WOULD LIKE TO.
LOCKED IN
RESPONDING TO SIGNIFICANT TASKS WITHOUT BECOMING EMOTIONALLY OVERWHELMED OR HITTING SNOOZE.
AUTOPILOT
NOT CONSCIOUSLY CONTROLLING OUR THOUGHTS, ATTITUDES, & BEHAVIORS. NOT MANAGING ADHD STRATEGICALLY. REACTIVE, PUTTING OUT FIRES AS THEY OCCUR.
PANIC MODE
RESPONSIVE TO OUR GREATEST PERCEIVED THREATS. EMPLOY SURVIVAL TACTICS—FIGHT, FLIGHT, FREEZE, FAWN.
CRASH ZONE
EMOTIONS BECOME EVEN MORE INTENSE. UNCONTROLLABLE, UNREASONABLE, & WILLING TO DESTROY OTHERS & SELF. OBSESSIONS TAKE OVER.
A STATE OF PERPETUAL "PRESENCE"
A QUIET Mind AND AT PEACE
AWAKE IN OUR MIND, HEART, & BODY
OPEN TO OURSELVES AND OUR ENVIRONMENT
PRESENT IN A NON-REACTIVE STATE
UNCONSCIOUS
PRODUCTIVE
SLOW DOWN
FAILURE
STUPID
ANXIETY
EMOTIONAL VOICE
PROJECTING CHAOS
LOW HEALTH
DESTRUCTIVE
ACTUALIZING
THE POSITIVE POTENTIAL
NOT ONE THE
MINDFULNESS
DEFENSIVE
HAPPY AND IN TUNE
STRATEGIES TO KEEP YOURSELF STEADY
FEELING GOOD
WALKING A TIGHTROPE
ANY UNEXPECTED BUMP COULD THROW US INTO A SPIRAL, BREAKING OUR AUTOPILOT SYSTEM.
PUTTING OUT FIRES AS THEY OCCUR
FIGHT Flight FREEZE
WILLING TO DESTROY SELF & OTHERS
PANIC
BULLDOZE YOUR RELATIONSHIPS

11

Who Am I, Really? (And Why ADHD Makes It Tricky)

Sometimes it might feel like who you are changes depending on the room you're in. At home, you might be "the difficult one." Around extended family, you're the quiet one who barely speaks. With one group of friends, you're the sarcastic one; with another, the responsible one. And when you're alone, you feel like a different version altogether—creative, curious, and thoughtful in ways nobody else sees. Each version feels true in the moment, but none of them quite add up to the whole you.

Leo described it this way: "At school, I'm that kid who never has his stuff. Teachers don't even bother asking anymore—they just assume I forgot. At soccer, I'm the hype guy, cracking jokes, keeping the energy up. But the second I'm quiet, people are like, 'What's wrong with you?' I can't even chill for one practice without everyone freaking out. Online, it's different. In my Discord, I'm the one explaining stuff–what games just dropped and how to beat a level."

Leo's still figuring out who he is–like most people do during their teens and early twenties. With ADHD, though, your sense of self can feel especially unstable. Your brain reacts strongly to what's happening around you, so even minor changes–like a teacher's comment, a friend's mood, or the vibe in the room–can alter how you behave. Sometimes you might not even realize why you're acting differently. Over time, all these shifts can make you wonder which version of yourself is the real one.

The challenging part of having ADHD is that your identity doesn't always feel like one continuous story. It can seem fragmented into moments–pieces that don't easily come together to form a bigger picture. That's why it can sometimes feel like you're changing shapes instead of staying steady.

Why Identity Feels Like a Moving Target

With ADHD, it can feel like your sense of self keeps glitching. One day you feel on top of things, the next you barely recognize yourself. Time feels blurry. You adjust to the room, but feedback feels loaded with negative messages. Shame builds up. Emotions take control. And sometimes memory drops parts of your story. All of this can leave your identity skipping between frames so quickly that you're unsure which one is the real you.

Time Doesn't Exist: How Time Blindness Affects Identity

Research shows that with ADHD, it's harder to judge how much time has passed, to hold on to future plans, and to picture what's coming next.* When time feels fuzzy like this, it shapes how you experience yourself over time.

Jayden explained, "It kinda feels like I only exist right now. But even that version of me doesn't always stick. Once the moment's gone, it fades like it was never really there. Past Me disappears, Future Me doesn't feel real, and even Present Me feels temporary."

If the past feels vague and the future is hard to picture, it's tough to feel like the same person all the way through.

- **What's one time you thought, *I'll do that later*, and "later" never really showed up? How did missing that moment change the way you talked to yourself?**

Ghosted by Your Own Goals: How Working Memory Issues Affect Identity

Working memory slips add another twist to figuring out who you really are. With ADHD, you might forget the plans and goals that are supposed to guide you. One day you're fired up to start something new, and a week later it's like that version of you vanished. You forget what you wanted, why you cared, or even that you made the plan in the first place.

Sofia told me she gets excited about new plans, but then the intention slips away. "I'll decide I'm going to start something like running, and I'm actually excited about it," she explained. "But then I forget to do it. I mean, I totally forget that I was planning on running that day."

* Radek Ptacek et al., "Clinical Implications of the Perception of Time in Attention Deficit Hyperactivity Disorder (ADHD): A Review," *Medical Science Monitor* 25 (May 26, 2019): 3918–24, https://doi.org/10.12659/MSM.914225.

For her, the frustration wasn't about not sticking to her exercise plan. Losing track of goals can feel like losing track of yourself because, as Sophia says, "The 'me' who decided yesterday and the 'me' today don't always feel connected."

- **Describe a goal you were really excited about but later forgot. What happened, and what did you tell yourself afterward?**

Masks and Mirrors: How People-Pleasing and Masking Affect Identity

People-pleasing isn't about being fake; it's about protecting yourself. When you live with ADHD, you may be especially aware of whether you're being accepted or about to face rejection. Adjusting yourself to fit in can feel like armor: If you keep teachers calm, smooth things over at home, or mirror your friends' energy, maybe you'll avoid conflict or embarrassment. In the moment, it works. But the more you change yourself for others, the harder it gets to recognize which version is truly you.

Masking takes people-pleasing to a new level. Instead of adjusting how much you show of yourself, you start hiding entire parts so no one notices slips, fidgets, or moments that feel like "too much." With ADHD, masking can mean holding back questions even when you're confused or pretending you're calm when you're overwhelmed. It can keep you out of trouble and help you blend in, but it also drains your energy and leaves you wondering if people like *you* or just the masks you wear.

As Zahra described, she keeps shape-shifting–talking about anime with school friends "even though I don't actually care that much," going quiet at home "because my sister is such a mess," and increasing her sarcasm with theater friends to match their energy–only to later wonder, *Was that actually me, or the version everyone else needed?*

People-pleasing and masking may help you get through a moment, but afterward, they can leave you unsure if anyone saw the real you–including you.

- **Describe a time you changed how you acted to fit the people around you. Which parts of the real you came through, and which parts got left out or changed?**

Big Emotions Spills: How Emotional Regulation Affects Identity

Another reason identity can feel slippery with ADHD is the intensity of emotions. The brain's braking system doesn't always slow strong feelings, so they can hit hard and take over. Excitement can come out as laughing too loudly or talking too fast, and suddenly you're "the over-the-top one." If your feelings get hurt easily, you're "the sensitive one." In those moments, the feeling takes center stage and seems like it defines your entire self.

Zahra told me, "When I blow up at my brother, it's not just, 'I was mad.' My parents act like I'm an angry person. But that's not the whole me. It's just what came out in that moment."

That's how emotional flooding works. One feeling becomes so intense it overshadows everything else. With

ADHD, those signals are stronger and more persistent, making it easy for you—and those around you—to confuse a passing emotion with your permanent personality. The cost is that identity starts to feel like whatever emotion shows up the loudest, instead of being the full range of who you are.

▶ **Describe a moment when a strong emotion took control. How did other people respond to you, and how did that affect how you saw yourself?**

Looping Negative Feedback: How External Feedback Affects Identity

Other people's reactions and comments can influence how you see yourself. You probably remember some negative comments like, "You're late again," "Stop blurting," "You're so extra." Even if they seem small or throwaway, they can replay in your mind. Over time, those echoes begin to feel like proof that this is who you are, even if it's not the whole story.

Lena told me that even when teachers praise her work, her mind skips over the good comments and locks onto the minor mistakes. As she put it, "I focus on the details that I screwed up, even if I got an A."

Studies show that when you have ADHD, your brain pays extra attention to mistakes. The "error signals" in your brain go off louder and take longer to quiet down, so criticism hangs around.* Additionally, memories tied to embarrass-

* Catharina S. van Meel et al., "Telling Good from Bad News: ADHD Differentially Affects Processing of Positive and Negative Feedback During Guessing," *Neuropsychologia* 43, no. 13 (2005): 1946–54, https://doi.org/10.1016/j.neuropsychologia.2005.03.018.

ment or mistakes tend to stick more firmly than those that are neutral. That's why one harsh comment can loop in your head for days, while ten kind ones disappear almost right away. When that happens, it's easy to start accepting other people's negative comments as the truth about who you are—even when they tell only part of the story.

- What's one comment that keeps replaying in your mind?

- When you get feedback, what does your brain zoom in on first—the mistake or the praise?

- What part of the story about you might that comment be leaving out?

The Ultimate Troll: How Shame Affects Identity

Criticism from others can hurt, but shame is what happens when your brain takes that hurt and turns it inward. Instead of stopping at "I messed that up," shame turns the words into "That's just who I am."

With ADHD, this jump can happen faster because of emotional tagging. When something embarrassing or painful occurs, your brain slaps a big "remember this" sticker on it. That tag hangs on, making the moment seem bigger than it really was. Over time, a single mistake can start to look like a personality trait—or even your entire identity.

Maya told me, "I forgot to text my grandma, and my brain went straight to 'I'm a terrible granddaughter.'"

Shame doesn't just hurt in the moment; it rewrites the story you tell yourself about who you are. It tricks you into believing the worst version of yourself. But here's the truth: Mistakes are events, not definitions. They don't decide your identity. You do.

- What is one negative comment that keeps replaying in your head? How has hearing it on repeat changed the way you see yourself? Is this accurate?

- Write about a compliment you had trouble believing. How might your picture of yourself be different if you let it stick?

- Tell about a time when a small mistake made you feel like a bad person. What happened, and what did your brain say about you afterward?

- If you retold that moment as "I messed up" instead of "I am messed up," how would the story about you change?

Finding You

All of this–time blindness, forgotten goals, shape-shifting to fit in, emotional flooding, replaying negatives, and piling on shame–makes it hard to hold on to a steady sense of who you are. The pieces are real, but ADHD scatters them so it feels like your identity keeps glitching.

In the next chapters, we'll explore a better way to build identity by anchoring yourself to what stays steady underneath: your own values, strengths, roles, and interests.

Values are what matter most to you–what you want to stand for no matter where you are. Strengths are the abilities you lean on, like creativity, humor, determination, or empathy. Roles are the parts you play in life, like student, sibling, teammate, or friend. Interests are the things that light you up and keep you grounded, like music, fashion, or art. Put them together, and you start to see a clearer picture of the real you–not only the version other people notice in the moment.

12

Dropping the Bricks, Carrying the Gear

Imagine carrying around a backpack that's already too full. Inside are all the "shoulds" people hand you: *Get straight A's. Join the team. Be organized. Calm down.*

Then come the judgments, tossed in like bricks: *You talk too much. You're too quiet. You're too much. You're not enough. Why can't you focus? Why are you so sensitive? Why can't you just be normal?* Each one digs in, making the straps bite into your shoulders.

After a while, even small comments or little mistakes feel like extra weight. Zahra knew that feeling when her mom sighed and said, "You forgot your water bottle for practice again." On its own, no big deal. For Zahra, it landed like another brick: *You forgot—again.*

Take a moment with the "What's in Your Backpack?" sidebar and notice what's been slipping into your backpack.

What's in Your Backpack?

Imagine your backpack.

- What "shoulds" have people tossed in there?
- What judgments weigh you down? (For example: *You're too loud. You'll never get it together.*)
- Which things reflect who you really are, and which are just expectations other people dumped in your bag?
- Write down a few of the expectations or judgments you're carrying, or draw your backpack and label each one inside it. Then imagine setting down just one of those bricks. How much lighter would it feel?

Values

Values are the gear you pack on purpose–the things that give strength to the load you carry. They remind you of the kind of person you want to be, the life you want to create.

A value is your "why"–the steady reason behind what you do. It's what turns a routine action into something that matters.

If you value learning, you don't cram dates for a history test; you want to understand the story behind them.

If you value creativity, you're drawn to games that let you design and explore instead of grind through levels.

If you value friendship, you make time to check in on your friends, even when life is packed.

Nico figured this out during a group project. When one teammate slacked off, he fumed, "I had to do everything. It's not right." At first, he thought he was angry about the extra work. But as he reflected, he realized it wasn't the workload. It was the unfairness. "I don't mind working hard," he said. "I just can't stand when people don't pull their weight." Fairness was part of his gear. When someone stomped on it, it felt like they'd ripped through his backpack and scattered what mattered most.

You already have values like that too. Some have grown out of proud moments when you felt alive or connected. Others have come from people you admire, like a teacher who treated everyone with respect or a friend who always kept their word. And sometimes values are shaped by negative experiences, like when someone hurts you and you decide, *I never want to treat people that way.*

Values aren't handed to you. They grow out of your choices, your experiences, and the kind of person you want to become. That's what makes them powerful—they belong to you.

Values vs. Goals

Goals and values sound similar, but they're not the same.

A goal is something you *do*. It's specific and measurable and has a finish line, like passing a history test or saving

Clues to What You Value

Think of a moment when you felt proud.

- **What were you doing?**

- **Who else was there?**

- **Which value might have been at work—creativity, kindness, fairness, courage? (You can peek at appendix B to give you ideas.)**

Now think of a time when something felt unfair or wrong.

- **What happened? Why did it bother you?**

- **Which value might have been stepped on?**

enough money for a new game. You complete it and move on.

A value is something you *live out*. It's steady and ongoing and doesn't get crossed off a list.

Goals come and go. Values are the direction you keep walking in.

Goals and Values

Think back on a goal you've set recently.

- What was the goal? (Big or small—anything counts.)
- Did you reach it, or did it not turn out as you had hoped?
- Underneath that goal, what value might have been driving it? (For example: *I wanted to get an A on my project because I value learning and effort. I wanted to make the team because I value connection and teamwork.*)
- Can you think of another way to live out that same value, even if the original goal changed?

Zahra discovered this when she tried out for her school's soccer team. Her goal was to make the roster. When she didn't, she was crushed. For weeks, she told herself she'd failed.

Eventually, she realized that what she truly wanted wasn't the jersey but the connection. "I just wanted to be with my friends," she said. Connection was the true value behind her goal. Once she understood that, she found other ways to experience it, like joining a local club team.

That's the power of knowing your values. A missed goal can feel like failure, but if you uncover the value underneath, you'll see other paths forward. The goal may shift, but the value stays steady.

Why Values Matter for an ADHD Brain

Values give your brain a reason to care. Loading the dishwasher might feel pointless, unless you connect it to family and think, *I want to help my parents.* A group project might feel draining, unless you tie it to creativity (*I want to present this in a fresh way*) or fairness (*I want everyone's voice to be heard*).

Values won't magically turn a chore into your favorite activity, but they can change how it feels. Instead of "random

How Values Activate Your Brain

The prefrontal cortex helps you zoom out and connect your choices to the bigger picture. With ADHD, the prefrontal cortex doesn't always switch on. But when you link a task to a value, that system wakes up and partners with your motivation circuits. That's what makes it easier to start–and to keep going.

task," your brain sees "part of my story." And that shift can be the difference between feeling stuck and moving forward.

What Do You Value?

When you ask yourself, *What matters to me?*, you start to notice the difference between what weighs you down and what propels you forward. Understanding your values helps you distinguish what is genuinely yours from the "shoulds" others have added to your backpack. When you can identify your values, you're less likely to be diverted by expectations and more likely to follow a path that feels authentic to you.

Look at the values list in appendix B and circle the ones that stand out. Don't overthink it. Notice which ones seem like they belong in your list. Some may overlap with those of your friends or family, and others may be completely different. That mix is what makes your list unique.

Most of the values on the list will sound good, but you can't carry them all. If you try, they stop feeling like real values and start feeling like more "shoulds." That's like stuffing every possible item into your backpack until it's so heavy you can't move.

Once you've circled your values, go back and narrow them down to your top three to five. Think of these as your essentials—the things you want to carry with you right now. They'll help you figure out your next move when life feels messy. And remember, your backpack isn't locked. You can swap values in and out as you grow.

If choosing feels overwhelming, check out the directions at the end of appendix B to help clarify your thinking.

Living Your Values

Living your values isn't always easy. The most challenging moments–when you're mad, hurt, hungry, exhausted, or ready to give up–are often the ones that show what actually matters to you. They're things you wrestle with and keep choosing, even when every part of you wants to quit.

Ali found this out after a fight with her sister. Her sister had grabbed her headphones without asking, then tossed them on the floor when she was done.

"She never listens. Ever. And of course she gets away with it, like always. It's not fair," Ali ranted. "I yelled at her–I mean, really yelled. Then I slammed my door. Whatever, she deserved it."

"Sounds like you felt disrespected," I said. "Respect was at the top of your values list, right?"

"Yeah!" she shot back.

"It sounds like respect matters to you, but that moment didn't really line up with it."

Honestly, Ali had a point. Living your values is hardest when other people aren't living them with you. But that's exactly when they matter most–in the heat of a fight, when your emotions are loud and every part of you wants to toss your values out the window.

That's also what makes your values powerful. They're not just nice words you agree with when life is calm. They're reminders of the kind of person you want to be when things get messy. You won't always get it right–and that's okay. Even noticing the gap, like Ali realizing she valued respect but wasn't showing it, is a step toward living closer to what matters.

Think about your top three to five values. Then ask yourself:

- How do I already live this value out? (For example: *I value fairness, so I speak up when someone's left out.*)

- How could I use it more often? (For example: *I value creativity, so I could sketch during study breaks instead of just scrolling.*)
- When have I missed this value, and what did I learn? (For example: *I value respect, but I lost it on my sister. It showed me I need to slow down before I react.*)

Write down a few examples for each of your values. The more you connect them to your actions, the more they become like gear you've chosen on purpose—the things in your backpack that give you strength when everything else feels heavy.

More Than Just Words

Values are the gear you choose to carry when life throws you distractions, detours, and emotional curveballs. They remind you of the kind of person you want to be, even when life feels chaotic.

The clearer you are about what truly matters, the easier it is to drop the "shoulds" and judgments that never belonged to you in the first place. Each time you pause, notice the gap, and take even a small step that reflects your values, you lighten your load and strengthen yourself for the road ahead.

Over time, your backpack shifts. It's no longer packed with other people's bricks; it's filled with the essentials you chose, steady and grounding, always there when you need them most.

In the next chapter, we'll look at your strengths, your roles, your interests, and the way others see you. Together with your values, these lenses give you a fuller picture of who you are—and who you're becoming.

13

The Real You, Piece by Piece

Identity isn't one label. It's built piece by piece. Each part adds something to the bigger picture of who you are.

In the last chapter, you uncovered your values—the "why" that guides what matters most. But that's only the beginning. To see the full picture, you also need to look at your strengths, your roles, and your interests. Think of it like building a profile:

Values are your "About Me"—the steady background settings that shape what feels right.

Strengths are your highlight reel—the qualities that keep showing up.

Roles are your tags—student, friend, sibling, teammate.

Interests are your playlists—the things that keep pulling your attention.

Put together, these show the steady threads running through your life—the pattern that makes up the real you.

Finding Your Strengths

Another piece of identity comes from your strengths—the qualities you're naturally good at or the skills you've built over time. Strengths aren't just grades, trophies, or being "the best." They're things like creativity, humor, determination, empathy, or problem-solving.

With ADHD, strengths often fade into the background. Your brain runs a blooper reel on loop—replaying the missed homework and skipping the essay you nailed. That's why naming your strengths matters. It balances what ADHD leaves out.

Values and strengths often go hand in hand. Values are what matter; strengths are how you live them out. If loyalty is your value, dependability might be your strength. When you see these pairing up, a larger pattern appears. You notice the qualities that consistently appear throughout your life.

Jayden thought of himself as "the kid who never finishes stuff." He'd started a dozen projects—comic sketches, coding experiments, even a backyard garden—only to lose steam halfway. But in art class, a teacher said, "You've got a knack for seeing connections other people miss." That changed the way he saw himself. Jayden realized his strength wasn't about finishing projects; it was creativity. Even when things didn't get finished, his ideas sparked new directions.

Your strengths are there even if no one calls them out. They're the parts of you that keep showing up, no matter the role—proof of what you bring with you wherever you are.

Strengths Menu

Look through these categories and circle or highlight anything that sounds like you. Narrow it down to five to seven strengths, and describe how you use these strengths on a regular basis.

People Strengths

Caring (I look out for people)
Compassionate (I feel for people and want to help)
Empathetic (I notice how people feel and care about it)
Friendly (I'm easy to talk to and approachable)
Inclusive (I make sure people don't feel left out)
Kind (I treat people with respect and care)
Loyal (I stand by my people, no matter what)
Peacemaker (I calm drama or stop fights)
Supportive (I show up when people need me)
Trustworthy (People know I'll keep their confidence)

Creative Strengths

Artistic (I make things look or sound cool)
Creative (I come up with new ideas or ways to do things)
Curious (I like exploring, asking questions, and learning stuff)
Imaginative (I picture things in new ways)
Visionary (I see the big picture or future possibilities)

Action Strengths

Adventurous (I'm up for trying new things)
Brave (I face hard stuff, even when I'm nervous)
Determined (I don't give up, even when it's tough)
Energetic (I bring a lot of energy to the room)
Quick-thinking (I can react fast in the moment)
Risk-taker (I go for it, even when I don't know the outcome)

Thinking Strengths

Insightful (I notice patterns or truths others miss)
Problem-solving (I figure things out when they go wrong)
Resourceful (I use what I have to make things work)
Self-aware (I notice what I'm feeling or doing)
Tech-savvy (I get how to use or fix technology)

Steady Strengths

Adaptable (I roll with changes)
Calm under pressure (I stay steady when things get intense)
Consistent (I keep showing up)
Flexible (I can pivot when plans change)
Honest (I say what I really think)
Hopeful (I believe things can get better)
Independent (I figure things out on my own)
Open-minded (I hear new ideas without shutting them down)
Optimistic (I look for the bright side)
Organized (I keep track of stuff or systems)
Patient (I can wait things out without snapping)
Reliable (People can count on me)
Respectful (I treat people the way I want to be treated)

Leadership Strengths

Charismatic (People are drawn to me)
Collaborative (I work well with others)
Confident (I believe in myself, or fake it until I do)
Cooperative (I can follow through when I'm on a team)
Encouraging (I hype people up when they need it)
Leader (I guide groups forward)
Motivating (I inspire or encourage others)

Developing Your Strengths

Spotting your strengths is only the beginning. They grow when you start using them in different places. Maybe you chose determined. At first, you only notice it at soccer practice, when you keep running drills after everyone else is tired. Then you try it somewhere new, like sticking with a tough math problem instead of giving up right away. Think of it like adding experience points to a skill in a game: Every time you use determination, even in small ways, it levels up.

Adding Experience Points

Choose one strength you circled in the Strengths Menu.

- Write down one place you already use it.

- Write down one new place you could try using it this week.

- Ask yourself, *Is there a strength I want to build? What's one small step I could try?*

- At the end of the week, jot a quick note: Did it feel natural? Hard? Helpful?

Some strengths don't come naturally at first. You have to build them. Sofia felt that way about confidence. "I'd think of something in class, but then I'd convince myself it was dumb," she said. Her first step was small: speaking up once a week, even if her voice shook. It was awkward, but over time she began to believe her ideas were worth hearing. "I still get nervous," she said, "but I don't shut myself down before I even try. I know my voice deserves a spot in the room."

Strengths grow like that—in small steps, practiced over time. The more you try them in new situations and notice how they feel, the stronger they get. What once felt impossible can become a strength you trust.

The Roles You Play

Another way to understand yourself is by examining the roles you assume—student, sibling, teammate, gamer, friend, worker, volunteer. You likely have more roles than you realize. They can serve as mirrors revealing who you're becoming.

Roles connect you to others and prove you belong, giving you feedback and perspective you can't get alone. They are also places to experiment. In one setting you might take initiative; in another you might hang back and listen. Over time, those experiments help you figure out what feels authentic. That freedom to try, shift, and grow is part of how you piece together your identity.

Roles shape you too. They push you to build habits, handle feedback, and stretch in ways you might not choose on your own. Even when they feel frustrating, they reveal steady patterns—like loyalty that shows up with friends, or humor that carries across groups.

Maya told me about her role on the debate team. "At first, I was just 'the backup,' the kid they put in when someone else couldn't make it," she said. "It felt like proof that nobody thought I was good enough." Over time, though, she leaned into preparation. She researched extra cases, asked coaches for feedback, and became the one people turned to when things got complicated. "I'm still not the loudest voice," she explained, "but I know I'm the reliable one. I bring something the team needs."

Maya realized that roles aren't fixed; they can grow. By developing her role, she discovered she could be both prepared and dependable. Those traits started to spill into other parts of her life, like group projects and friendships.

That's why roles matter. Roles aren't boxes. They're mirrors and training grounds that reflect back pieces of you. Understanding them helps you see which parts belong to you, which parts were handed to you, and how the real you shows up across all of them.

But who you are isn't only what others expect from you. It's also influenced by what you decide for yourself—your interests.

Think about one of your roles—student, friend, sibling, teammate, performer, gamer.

- **What have you learned from it?**

- **How has it helped you grow or develop a strength you didn't notice before?**

Following Your Own Curiosity

Interests are what grab your attention. They can help define who you are. They're what you choose when no one else is assigning you a role. Think of the books you pick up, the rabbit holes you fall into online, the music you replay on loop, or the hobbies you sink hours into without noticing the time.

With ADHD, interests can bounce around. One month you're sketching every day, the next you're practicing guitar, and later you're trying out 3D printing. It might feel random, but it's your curiosity testing doors and finding what excites you.

It's easy to get stuck in the Blue zone of the Solve-It Grid—the low-effort place you slip into when schoolwork, chores, or routines feel like a drag. That's when you drift into habits that pass time but don't give anything back, like endless scrolling or zoning out on YouTube. You aren't really developing an interest.

Green, the zone where your true interests usually live, takes more effort at first but recharges you. Even ten minutes of baking, shooting hoops, or playing guitar can turn "I wasted another night" into "I actually built something today."

For Darius, after school always looked the same: Flop on the couch and scroll TikTok until dinner.

"Does that help you reset?" I asked.

He shrugged. "I guess. Yeah, for a while."

"What if you tried using that time for one of your interests?"

So Darius picked up his guitar, even if it was only for ten minutes. At first, it felt awkward, but after a week it became his reset button. "By the time I ate dinner, I actually had more energy," he said.

Interests matter because they often activate your strengths. If you love gaming, maybe you've built strategy and problem-solving skills. If you're into music, maybe you've developed persistence through practice. If you're into fashion or thrifting, maybe creativity is one of your quiet superpowers. Interests can even grow into roles. Being a gamer, a musician, or an artist usually starts with simply being curious.

You don't have to stick with every interest forever. Some will fade, and others will surprise you by sticking. The point isn't to turn them all into career plans. It's worth noticing what draws you in, because those magnetic pulls—and those Green activities—show glimpses of the real you.

You Are an Interesting Person

Your interests don't have to be lifelong passions to matter. It's easy to forget that your mix of interests makes you unique. Try this:

- Write down three things that have grabbed your attention in the past month (big or small).
- Circle one. Ask yourself, *What does this interest say about me?*
- Imagine explaining this interest to someone else. How would it show them that you're an interesting person?

When Life Pushes Back

It's easy to name your values, strengths, and roles when life is calm. The real test is when things get messy—when a teacher calls you out in front of the class, when friends push you to go along with something you don't believe, or when

Testing Your Identity

Think about a time when your values, strengths, or roles got tested. Write a few quick notes:

- **What happened? (For example: *A teacher called me "lazy" because I missed an assignment.*)**

- **What did this situation test?**
    - Value (like honesty, loyalty, independence)
    - Strength (like humor, determination, creativity)
    - Role (like student, sibling, teammate, friend)

- **How did you react? (Did you go along, push back, shut down, or find another way?)**

- **What does your reaction tell you about what matters to you? If this happened again, what would you want to keep doing, and what would you do differently?**

ADHD makes it harder to show up the way you want. Those moments shape who you're becoming.

Sometimes you don't think about who you are at all. Other times you slip into an identity someone else hands you: *the smart one*, *the lazy one*. And sometimes you experiment. It can feel chaotic, but that's part of figuring yourself out.

Maya told me, "I used to just go along with whatever my friends wanted, even if I didn't like it. The first time I said no, I was low-key terrified–but also kind of proud. Like, wait . . . this is actually me." That moment mattered because it wasn't about pleasing anyone else. It was about Maya finally hearing her own voice.

Identity isn't one label forever. It's the steady parts–your values, strengths, roles, and interests–that show up again and again. The more you think about them, the more you'll believe, *This is me.*

14

When Your Brain Tells You That You Don't Belong

You send a text: *You free later?*

Ten minutes. No reply.

Twenty. Still nothing.

An hour. Your chest tightens.

Your brain skips *They're busy* and jumps straight to *I messed up. They hate me.*

By the time your phone finally buzzes, you've already built the story: *They don't actually like me. I said something dumb. I ruin everything.*

Even the smallest pause, the tiniest frown, or a casual "We need to talk" can set everything off. Your nervous system hits the alarm instantly, reacting before you've had a chance to think.

That overwhelming reaction has a name: rejection sensitive dysphoria (RSD)—when your brain treats a moment of possible rejection as proof you don't belong.

Not everyone with ADHD feels RSD, but many do. Neuroscience studies show social rejection activates some of the same brain pathways as physical pain. That's why it can land like a punch, even if no one actually rejected you.

Once RSD kicks in, your whole system reacts before your Butler brain can catch up. Your limbic system—the part that handles emotions—slams the panic button the second it senses negative feelings aimed in your general direction. Meanwhile, your prefrontal cortex (the Butler) is slow to respond to the commotion.

RSD doesn't hit in just one corner of life. It can sneak in anywhere—friends making plans without you, a teacher's tone that feels sharp, a group chat that goes quiet, a coach's feedback in practice. The situations look different, but the reaction inside feels the same: a sudden flood of panic, shame, or self-blame that's way bigger than the moment itself.

The Things That Sting

For most people with ADHD, it isn't always the big stuff like breakups or huge fights. More often, it's the small daily moments that land harder than expected.

Zahra told me, "If I hear people at school making plans and my name doesn't come up, my mind goes full detective. I'll replay every conversation—Did I annoy them? Did they leave me out on purpose?—until I've convinced myself I don't belong. Later, I find out it wasn't even a big deal, but I've already spent hours tearing myself apart."

For Jayden, his RSD can erupt when a teacher tells him that she needs to talk to him. "My stomach flips. I don't even hear the rest. It could be something simple like, 'We need to move your seat so that you can see better.' But in my head, I'm already failing, already disappointing everyone."

Leo notices RSD more with his team. "If the coach yells at me, I can't just shake it off. Even if he's yelling at everyone, I take it personally."

Survival Modes: Fight, Flight, Freeze, or Fawn

When RSD hits, your body reaches for old survival modes—automatic ways your brain and body try to protect you when something feels like a threat. Think of it as your nervous system's emergency playbook: You fight back, run away, freeze in place, or try to smooth things over. If you ran into a bear in the woods, those modes would kick in. You might try to scare it off (fight), sprint away (flight), stand still (freeze), or throw it your snack and hope it leaves you alone (fawn). With people, it works the same way.

Zahra goes into fight mode when she feels left out. Her first instinct is to fire off a cutting text or make a comment she instantly regrets.

Other times it might be a flight reaction. Jayden says if he thinks someone's disappointed in him, he'll stop answering texts for a while.

Leo freezes. He describes going blank when the coach calls him out. He's there, but it's like he can't think or move, replaying the moment instead of playing.

And then there's a fawn response. Maya tries to keep everyone calm, offering to help or overapologizing so no one stays upset.

All of these reactions are automatic, but they often turn a tough moment into something that feels way bigger than it actually is.

How Do You React?

Think about the last time you experienced RSD.

- **Did you fight—yell, snap, or get defensive?**

- **Did you take flight—ghost, avoid, or pretend it didn't matter?**

- **Did you freeze—go blank, shut down, or zone out?**

- **Did you fawn—overapologize or people-please to calm things down?**

There's no "right" answer here. Just noticing your pattern is the first step toward change.

The Stories We Create

Most of the time, your reaction isn't just about the fact; it's about the story your brain creates around it. The story forms so quickly that you don't even notice it happening, but it influences how you respond. As you look back, it's helpful to ask, *What story was I believing when I reacted that way?*

Zahra lashed out with a text because the story in her head was *They don't want me.* As she heard her friends make plans without her, her brain jumped to *They left me out on purpose.* By the time she hit send, she had already built a case against herself—remembering times she'd talked too much, laughed too loudly, or felt like the "extra" in the group.

Jayden ghosted his friend because his story was *I already messed everything up.* One unanswered message spiraled into *They're ignoring me because they don't want to deal with me.* Instead of checking in, he withdrew, then criticized himself for disappearing—proof, in his mind, that he was the problem all along.

Leo froze on the field because his story was *The coach thinks I'm a failure.* A single correction during practice snowballed into *Everyone can see I'm blowing it. I shouldn't even be out here.* His body stiffened under the weight of that story, which only made him feel like the coach's words were right.

Maya overapologized because her story was *It's my job to keep everyone calm.* When her friends argued, she jumped in with extra offers to help and even apologized for things that weren't hers to fix. Later, she worried that people only valued her as the peacekeeper and not for who she really was.

The story you tell yourself feels true, and the survival response can make it feel even more real. You lash out, go silent, freeze, or overapologize—and afterward, your reaction itself seems to confirm that the story was right all along.

Noticing the story you created helps you understand what happened. The more clearly you can identify the story, the more control you have to change it next time.

Once your brain locks onto a story, it stops treating the moment as neutral information and starts treating it as a threat. That's the opening RSD is waiting for.

Fact vs. Add-On

- **Write down the fact. (What really happened?)**

- **Describe the add-on story. (What did you tell yourself it meant?)**

- **Challenge the add-on. (What evidence do I have? Could there be another explanation? What would I tell my best friend if they believed this?)**

RSD takes a single moment of rejection and spins an add-on that feels much bigger than the fact itself. The fact is simple: *I didn't get picked. They didn't text me back. I got a C on that test.* RSD piles on with extra messages: *I'll never be good enough. They don't like me. I'm stupid.* Suddenly you're not reacting to what happened. You're reacting to the harsh remix your thoughts created.

Breaking the Loop

You can't always stop your brain from creating a story, but you can learn to pause long enough to catch the shift from fact to story. Think of it like hitting pause before the next episode autoplays. A quick stop gives you space to ask, *Do*

I want to keep watching this story, or do I want to swipe to something else?

Step 1: Spot the Jump from Fact to Story

Most of us don't notice when the jump happens; we realize it only after we've already reacted. Noticing it will get easier with practice. Pay attention to the words you use.

Fact: *They didn't text me back.*

Story: *They hate me.*

That one small shift is the moment your brain moves from reality to interpretation. Spotting it is the way to address RSD.

Jayden noticed his brain doing this one afternoon. The fact was *No text back*. The story was *I ruined everything*. Naming that jump gave him a second to breathe.

Step 2: Ask a Spell-Breaking Question

Once you notice the jump your mind made, drop in a question that snaps you out of the rejection trance. Try asking yourself:

What else could be true?

What part is fact, and what part is guesswork?

If my best friend told me this story, what would I say to them?

What do I not know yet?

These questions won't make the sting of rejection vanish, but they can crack the illusion and help you see the difference between what happened and what your brain added.

When Maya felt the urge to overapologize, she paused and asked herself, *What part of this argument is actually mine to fix?* That one question helped her step back and realize she was carrying more than she needed to.

Step 3: Name the Survival Mode

Fight, flight, freeze, fawn–these are your brain's automatic defense settings, ready to launch when something feels unsafe. Labeling the reaction gives you space. Instead of reacting, you're noticing that it happens.

Leo practiced saying his freeze moments out loud. Rather than thinking, *I'm a failure*, he said, "That was freeze mode kicking in." It helped him see his body was trying to protect him, even if freezing didn't really help in that moment.

Step 4: Try a Rewrite

Rewriting the story you told yourself doesn't mean making it unrealistically positive. It means shifting it into something more balanced and less punishing.

Instead of "I'm a failure," rewrite to "I made a mistake, but I can still learn."

Instead of "They're ignoring me," rewrite to "I don't know why they didn't reply–it might not be about me at all."

Zahra practiced rewriting by journaling. Her first draft thought was, "They don't want me." Then she tried a second version: "I don't know why they made plans without me, but it doesn't automatically mean I'm unwanted." It didn't erase the pain, but it gave her another perspective.

5 Steps to Break the RSD Loop

1. *Spot the jump.* Notice when your mind turns a fact into a story.
2. *Ask a spell-breaking question.* Slip in a question that cracks the illusion.
3. *Name the survival mode.* Label it fight, flight, freeze, or fawn. Naming it gives you space.
4. *Try a rewrite.* Shift the script into something more balanced and less punishing.
5. *Practice the pause.* Just one pause—even late—strengthens the skill and changes the ending.

Step 5: Practice the Pause

The pause isn't about fixing the feeling or forcing yourself to calm down. It's a moment to slow your reaction long enough to separate the fact from the story your brain is telling. Even a brief pause can interrupt the RSD loop and keep the story from taking over.

At first, you might notice the loop only after it has already happened—and that's okay. Reflecting afterward still builds the skill. The more you practice noticing the pattern, the sooner you'll start catching it in real time. Even a single pause during the loop can change how the story ends.

Zahra usually realized her overthinking hours later, replaying what she should have said. But one afternoon, in the middle of spiraling about a group chat, she caught herself and said, "Pause. I don't know what they meant." The worry didn't disappear, but the pause stopped the story from snowballing. Instead of firing off a text, she gave herself time to wait for more information.

That's what the pause does. It doesn't erase the emotion. It slows the momentum just enough to give you more choices about what comes next.

When It Really Is Rejection

Sometimes RSD makes you imagine rejection and spin it bigger than it is. But other times, the rejection isn't imagined; it's real. You didn't get the part. Your crush said no. Your friends truly did make plans without you. Teachers, coaches, and colleges will all hand out disappointing answers at some point.

When that happens, the sting is sharp. It can hit your whole system at once. Your stomach drops. Your throat tightens. Your thoughts spiral: *Everyone noticed. Everyone knows. Everyone's moving on without me.* Even when no one else is around, it can feel like you're standing under a spotlight with the whole world watching.

For some people, the ache fades in a day or two. But when you have ADHD, your nervous system can grip it like Velcro. A casual no from someone else can echo in your mind as if it's proof of your worth. That single moment replays in your head like a stuck video loop—every time just as vivid, every time just as personal.

So yes, it hurts. Sometimes the bravest thing you can do is admit it: "This hurts. I don't like how this feels." It's acknowledging what's happening in your body and mind. That can be enough to help your nervous system settle so you can move forward.

Long-Term Strategies: Building Rejection Muscles

The quick tools in this chapter can get you through an RSD storm in the moment. But if you want the waves to feel less overwhelming over time, you need to build what I call your "rejection muscles." Like any muscle, they grow gradually—through practice, support, and repetition.

One way to strengthen these muscles is by taking small risks. Go for the audition even if you're not sure you'll get the part. Share your idea in class even if it might flop. Every time you put yourself out there and survive a no, your nervous system learns that even though rejection hurts, it doesn't destroy you. Over time, the hits won't knock you down as far or for as long because you've trained for them.

Supportive relationships are another key piece. We all need safe people—friends, siblings, mentors—who take our feelings seriously. Sometimes a quick text—*My RSD is kicking in*—and a reply like, *I get it—you're okay*, can help you feel grounded again.

Professional help can also build long-term strength. ADHD-informed coaching and therapy can give you practical tools and a steady perspective. Therapists sometimes use cognitive behavioral therapy—a kind of thought training—to help you spot when your thoughts are jumping to the harshest possible conclusion and how to reframe them before they take over. ADHD coaches help you notice patterns, test strategies, and stick with what works. Having someone outside your own head reflect back what's fact and what's RSD can be a game changer.

Building rejection muscles doesn't mean rejection stops hurting. It means learning how to take the hit, recover, and keep moving instead of staying stuck. One text left on read doesn't erase who you are. One grade, one look, one no—it can sting, but it doesn't tell your whole story.

Rejection doesn't write your story. You do.

15

Now What?

You've reached the end of this book—but not the end of your story. ADHD can make life feel unpredictable, frustrating, even exhausting. It can also make life surprising, creative, and uniquely yours.

You've learned that ADHD isn't a weakness or a flaw. It's part of the way your brain is wired. Seeing that clearly lets you set down blame and start using strategies built for your mind, not against it.

This book has offered stories, tools, and new ways of understanding yourself. We've covered a lot, so here's a quick look back:

Chapter 1: *ADHD is real and brain-based.* It isn't laziness or lack of effort. It shows up as distractibility, impulsivity, working memory slips, and emotions that come in fast and strong. Understanding that gives you a more accurate way to see yourself.

Chapter 2: *Your brain thinks in pictures and metaphors.* Whether it's a raccoon in a hoodie or another image you invent, metaphors make hidden experiences visible and give you words to explain ADHD without shame.

Chapter 3: *Executive function challenges shape daily life.* If your brain is a mansion, the inconsistent Butler (prefrontal cortex) sometimes forgets what to do, while the Alarm System (limbic system) misfires. That explains working memory gaps, shutdowns, or meltdowns.

Chapter 4: *Divergent thinking is power—when you can steer it.* Your mind branches in bold, creative directions; it can also spiral into what-ifs. Balancing divergent thinking with convergent thinking and using simple cues keep you moving on purpose.

Chapter 5: *Fake power-ups masquerade as motivation but drain you.* Avoidance, perfectionism, anxiety, anger, and shame can push you forward briefly but leave wreckage behind. Swap them for real power-ups like curiosity sparks, mini wins, body doubling, reminders, and meaningful rewards.

Chapter 6: *Time doesn't play by the same rules in an ADHD brain.* "Now" and "later" don't feel evenly spaced, which makes plans disappear, tasks feel urgent only at the last second, and motivation swing wildly. Learning to externalize time with cues, starts, and structure helps you work with it instead of getting ambushed by it.

Chapters 7–8: *Energy isn't endless.* Some things take way more out of you than you expect, while others actually give energy back. The Solve-It Grid helps you spot unhelpful patterns—like the Need-for-Speed or getting stuck in Nothin'-but-Blue—and make choices that protect your energy.

Chapters 9–10: *Emotions are signals, not commands.* They arrive fast and strong but don't have to run the show.

The Emotional Health Ladder gives you ways to notice where you are and climb back up from spirals or shutdowns.

Chapter 11: *ADHD can blur your sense of self.* When your actions don't always match your intentions, it's easy to feel inconsistent or unsure of yourself. Naming your identity on purpose gives you something to hold on to when the rest of life gets loud.

Chapter 12: *Your values keep you grounded.* Even when motivation fades or emotions take control, knowing what matters to you provides a way to choose intentionally, not just react to the moment.

Chapter 13: *Your strengths, roles, and interests are a vital part of who you are.* They don't disappear just because follow-through is difficult or energy varies. Recognizing where they show up helps you understand yourself better and leverage what's already working.

Chapter 14: *Rejection can twist a moment into a belief that you don't belong.* Your brain can interpret a small cue—like silence, a look, or a change in tone—and turn it into proof that you're unwanted or excluded. Learning to recognize those extra thoughts helps you separate what actually happened from what your mind is making it mean.

Most importantly: *ADHD is only one part of your story.* It doesn't get to be the author. You do.

Shaping Your Story

Your ADHD story isn't something other people write about you; it's the way you understand your brain, your experiences, and what you do with them. All through this book, you've been shaping that story without necessarily realizing it—every time a metaphor clicked, a chapter called you out (in a good way), or a question made you think about yourself differently.

Take a minute to look back at what you learned and put some of it into your own words.

This book made me understand that . . .

This book made me hope that . . .

This book made me wish that . . .

This book made me decide that . . .

This book made me look at . . .

This book made me believe that . . .

This book made me remember that . . .

This book made me wonder if . . .

This book made me want to . . .

Now look back at what you wrote. Which lines matter most right now? What do they reveal about what you want to do next?

How to Advocate for Yourself

Advocacy is how you turn what you've learned into real life. Advocacy doesn't have to be big or dramatic. It starts with everyday moments where you speak up.

When you advocate for yourself, you free up energy that would otherwise get swallowed by silent struggling. Instead of burning brainpower trying to push through alone, you create more space for the things that actually matter to you. Speaking up also builds self-respect. Each time you ask for what helps, you prove to yourself that your needs aren't optional extras; they're real, and they deserve attention.

Advocacy also strengthens connection. People around you can't read your mind; they can only guess what you need unless you tell them. When you voice it, you give them the chance to see and support the real you. Over time, these moments become practice for the future. Speaking up in small ways now makes it easier to advocate in bigger spaces later—in jobs, friendships, and relationships, where your voice truly matters.

Most of the time advocacy is small: one sentence, one question, one boundary. But those small moments add up. Each one reminds your brain—and the people around you—that your needs are valid and worth taking seriously.

What Makes Speaking Up Hard

Even when you know what would help, saying it out loud can feel complicated. You may hesitate to advocate for yourself because of things like:

- *Worry about being judged.* You fear someone will think you're dramatic or making excuses.
- *Not wanting to stand out.* Blending in can feel safer than asking for something different.

- *Not knowing what to ask for.* You feel something's off, but you don't have the words yet.
- *Bad past experiences.* Maybe someone brushed you off, got annoyed, or laughed.

If any of that feels familiar, you're in good company. People who are great at advocating almost always started out nervous. The turning point isn't confidence; it's realizing your needs matter enough to voice them anyway.

What It Can Sound Like

Sometimes it helps to hear the kinds of words you're allowed to use. These are examples, not scripts you have to copy, but they show what self-advocacy can sound like in real life.

AT SCHOOL

"I do better when I have instructions in writing. Could you write this down or let me take a picture of the board?"

"I want to get this done on time, but I need the steps broken down. Can you help me figure out the first piece?"

"I lost track for a minute. Could you repeat the last part?"

WITH FRIENDS

"That came out wrong—I didn't mean to sound harsh. Can I try again?"

"I need a few minutes to calm down, then I want to talk."

"I'm sorry I forgot about our plans. It matters to me—can we reschedule?"

AT WORK

Whether it's your first job, volunteering, babysitting, or helping out at home, these can help:

"I can do a better job if I focus on one task at a time. Which one should I start with?"

"Could you leave me a checklist so I don't miss a step?"

"I know I messed up. Can you show me the right way so I can get it down?"

WITH FAMILY

"I'm not ignoring you—I'm overwhelmed. Can we talk in ten minutes?"

"Can you text me a reminder tonight so I don't forget?"

"I want you to understand what this feels like for me. Would you read this part of the book?"

What Helps When You Speak Up

When you advocate for yourself, a few things can make it easier:

Be specific so people know how to support you.

Speak with calm confidence—you're not asking for special treatment.

Focus on what helps you succeed, not on what's "wrong."

Practice saying the words out loud. Your brain needs reps to make it feel normal.

The more you use your voice, the more real it becomes—to you and to everyone around you.

Main Character Energy

Your story isn't finished. ADHD might be a recurring character in it, but it doesn't control the plot. You do.

Main character energy is showing up as yourself even when people don't fully get you. It's choosing curiosity instead of shame, persistence instead of panic, and connection instead of disappearance. It's remembering that setbacks aren't the end of anything–they're plot twists, not cancellation notices.

You don't have to play the sidekick in someone else's narrative. You are the main character. Your strengths, values, and voice set the direction. You get to decide what happens next.

And that part–the next part–belongs to you.

Appendix A

What About Medication?

If you have ADHD, chances are someone has brought up medication—maybe your doctor, a parent, a teacher, or even a friend. You might have heard:

- "Have you thought about medication?"
- "Do you *need* to take that every day?"
- "Don't you want to try harder before taking something?"

If those conversations have ever left you feeling judged, confused, or unsure, know that many others share this same struggle.

ADHD isn't just about behavior; it's about brain chemistry. The parts of your brain that handle focus, motivation, and self-control process dopamine and norepinephrine differently than most people's.

Medication doesn't "fix" ADHD, but it can give your brain more of what it needs to work the way you want it to. Some people describe taking their medication like putting on glasses for the first time: The world hasn't changed, but suddenly they can see it more clearly and interact with it more easily.

The right medication can make it easier to:

- start things instead of stalling for hours
- stick with tasks instead of getting constantly sidetracked
- shift your focus on purpose
- keep emotional surges from taking over
- finish what you meant to start

ADHD medications generally come in two types: stimulants, which act quickly, and nonstimulants, which take longer but may be a better fit for some people. Everyone's brain is different, so finding the right type, dose, and timing often takes some trial and error. That's normal–it doesn't mean the medication isn't working. It simply means you're still learning what your brain responds to.

Medication can help, but it isn't the whole picture. It won't organize your backpack, remember due dates, or magically manage your time. What it *can* do is make it easier to use the tools you're building, like planning your week, breaking tasks into steps, and asking for help when you need it.

Bottom line:

- If you're taking meds–great.
- If you're still figuring it out–that's valid.
- If you've tried meds and decided they're not for you–that's part of the journey too.

Your brain is worth caring for, and you deserve real support while you figure out what helps. What works for you right now might shift as you grow, and that's completely normal. Notice when your ADHD symptoms flare up, when they ease, and whether medication or other tools are making a difference. The more you understand how your brain works, the more power you have to choose strategies that actually make your life easier.

Appendix B

Need Help Making a Decision? Try the Values Auction

Circle the values below that jump out at you. Don't over-think it.

Adventure	Fairness	Kindness
Authenticity	Faith/Spirituality	Leadership
Balance	Family	Learning
Belonging	Friendship	Loyalty
Caring for others	Fun	Mental health
Community	Generosity	Nature/Environment
Connection	Growth	Perseverance
Courage	Helping others	Respect
Creativity	Honesty	Responsibility
Curiosity	Humor	Self-expression
Determination	Inclusion	Teamwork
Diversity	Independence	Trust
Equality	Justice	Add your own: ________________

Look at the values you circled and narrow your list to your top three to five. These are the essentials you want in your backpack right now. Remember, your values can shift as you grow. You can always swap things in or out later.

Values Auction

Still having a difficult time identifying what you value? Sometimes values become clearer when you have to choose between them. A Values Auction helps you notice which ideas, traits, and ways of living matter most to you. As you move through the activity, pay attention to the values you feel protective of, excited about, or unwilling to give up. Those reactions can reveal what is genuinely important to you.

Directions: You have 50 points to spend. Start by giving at least 10 points to each value you consider nonnegotiable—the ones you most want guiding your choices and relationships. Then divide the rest of your points among the other values that still matter to you.

Some values may not get enough points to make the cut, and that's okay. Not everything can fit in your backpack right now.

The values with the highest totals are likely your core values—the ones that matter most when life gets stressful, complicated, or messy.

Acknowledgments

It's been quite some time since I was a teenager, so I turned to teens and young adults for their perspectives on early versions of this manuscript. I am especially grateful to Ivan Wheland, Ziva Delph, Rebecca Cipcic, Katherine Gott, and others who read attentively, posed thoughtful questions, challenged what didn't ring true, and gave honest insights about what resonated—and what didn't. Your input made this book stronger and more authentic.

I also invited a few adults to read chapters—people who either work closely with teens and young adults or live alongside them daily.

Gena VanderMuelen, thank you for taking the time to talk through ideas with me. You are a thoughtful ADHD academic coach who genuinely cares about your students. Our conversations helped me clarify what needed to be stronger, clearer, and more practical. Your guidance shaped this book in meaningful ways.

Lollie Weeks, thank you for your review and for bringing both your professional wisdom and your lived experience with the young people in your life. Your comments confirmed the accuracy of the material and strengthened my confidence in what I was saying.

Lauren Rosier, my daughter, thank you for listening patiently as I talked through ideas, chapters, and timelines—and for occasionally raising an eyebrow when my deadlines felt . . . optimistic. Your steady presence, honest feedback, and encouragement as I wrote this on the back deck mean more to me than you know.

Andrea Doering, editorial director at Revell, thank you for your careful attention and thoughtful questions that strengthened this project. Our work together is a genuine collaboration.

Finally, Jessica English, senior editor at Revell, thank you for shaping this manuscript with such a keen eye. Your edits brought clarity and focus to these pages.

This book is better because of each of you.

TAMARA ROSIER, PhD, has worn a lot of hats–teacher, professor, college administrator, leadership coach, business owner, and ADHD coach. Along the way, she's spent years learning how ADHD actually shows up in real life, not just in textbooks. She has ADHD herself, so this work is personal.

Tamara is the founder of the ADHD Center of West Michigan, where she leads a team of coaches, therapists, and specialists who help kids, teens, adults, and families understand ADHD and learn how to work *with* their brains instead of fighting against them. She is also the author of *Your Brain's Not Broken* and *You, Me, and Our ADHD Family*. She cares deeply about helping people with ADHD feel understood and helping them build lives that really fit who they are.

CONNECT WITH TAMARA

ADHDCenterOfWestMichigan.com

Dr.TamaraRosier

https://www.linkedin.com/in/tamara-rosier-phd